What people ar
Choosing

Kat Tansey guides us in a meditation on the cat, tapping into ancient systems of attention that calm both the spirit and the flesh. Like a great cat, Choosing to Be *is a delight, a revelation, and a joy to curl up with.*
—**Meg Daley Olmert,** author of *Made For Each Other: The Biology of the Human-Animal Bond*

I found Choosing to Be *one of the better books on Zen or sitting practice. It's great—a wonderful book on meditation practice and our relationship with cats."*
—**Thom Hartmann,** radio show host and author of *Threshold : The Crisis of Western Culture*

Choosing to Be *is destined to affect millions of lives. This captivating and surprising story illuminates a surprising, yet simple pathway from inner turmoil to inner peace. Kat Tansey is every bit a wise as her eclectic team of Buddha masters.*
—**Mary E. Allen,** author of *The Power of Inner Choice*

Kat Tansey has crafted a book sure to be adored by all cat lovers. But even more importantly, this book is a must read for all caught up in a world spinning way too fast."
—**Dave Carpenter,** Peak Performance Show

We could all live more joyful lives if we learn the lessons in Choosing to Be.
—**Aurora Winter,** author of *From Heartbreak to Happiness*

Cats, meditation, and the quest for inner peace—what could be better! Choosing to Be *is an intriguing guide to Buddhist meditation and philosophy, with a special twist. Read it and be inspired."*
—**Carol Kline,** author of *Chicken Soup for the Cat Lover's Soul*

What readers are saying about
Choosing to Be . . .

This well written and very charming story convinced me meditation is as vital to our lives as food, water, and oxygen! Well done!
—Charles LeClair, Canada

I am so grateful to you for writing this book. It is a resource I will continue to draw on as I go through it again page by page, reflecting on the wisdom of this very wise Buddha master Maine Coon cat.
—Kim Lawrence, New York

I loved this book! Just reading it will lower your blood pressure.
—Jack Kimbell, Pennsylvania

The characters are wise, funny and charming, and kept me engaged to the end. As we follow the author's journey, the mystery surrounding Buddhist meditation is unraveled but the magic lingers on. It's a wonderful book.
—Marilyn Marbrook, New York

I highly recommend this book. It is engaging, funny, and full of practical wisdom.
—Carol Jefferies, Canada

A wonderful book—narrative drive, emotional power, original voices. The prose shines, and the story captivates from beginning to end.
—Kit Furey, Idaho

Choosing to Be

Lessons in Living
from a Feline
Zen Master

KAT TANSEY

FINDHORN PRESS

Choosing to Be
Lessons in Living from a Feline Zen Master

Copyright © 2008, 2010 by Kat Tansey

ISBN 978-1-84409-501-8

Cover design by Damian Keenan
Printed in the United States of America

1 2 3 4 5 6 7 8 9 18 17 16 15 14 13 12 11 10

Published by Findhorn Press
117-121 High Street
Forres IV36 1AB
Scotland, UK

t +44(0)1309 690582
f +44(0)131 777 2711
e info@findhornpress.com

www.findhornpress.com

Dedicated to
Poohbear and Catzenbear
—
the master and
his muse

green press
INITIATIVE

CONTENTS

Buddha Mind

FOREWORD

THE ONLY WAY I have found to access the resources of our vast and mostly unused powers is through our connection to our higher consciousness. The way to connect? Through our ability to quiet our mind.

Quieting our mind—that sounds easy, doesn't it? It is easy to say, "Okay, now, quiet your mind." Not so easy to do, though. Especially for us fast-paced Westerners, one of whom I used to be. I don't know about you, but I was brought up to feel a lull in the conversation embarrassing and silence unproductive. Besides, quiet might disturb or disrupt vast chasms of generations of denial and repression, and you don't want to go there . . .

Fortunately for us, when Kat Tansey, the author of *Choosing to Be,* learned how to quiet her mind and explore her vast chasms through Buddhist meditation, she came back to tell the tale and reveal the hidden treasure that awaits those who travel there—nothing less than inner peace. She created a travel guide for the rest of us.

This guide is what you have in your hands.

I want to assure you that Maine Coon cat Poohbear Degoonacoon, the wise and benevolent Buddha Master in Tansey's story, exists. I've had the great pleasure of spending many an enlightening afternoon with him and can attest to the fact he rivals Confucius for words of wisdom. I also have met and know Poohbear's daredevil sidekick—Maine Coon kitten Catzenbear, who is the embodiment of unspoiled Buddha nature, as well as quite a cut-up.

I suppose there may be some afraid to cross the line and

believe a higher-evolved Maine Coon cat and his kitten muse can teach his student, author Tansey, how to work with and learn from the Five Hindrances of Buddhist meditation.

To that I say, give yourself over. When Tansey learns that individual events are meaningless and insignificant and it is only through the *combination* of our experiences that we achieve an enlightened understanding, we learn it too. As she evolves as a meditator, learning to tolerate increasingly difficult memories and emotions, learning to explore rather than repress, we learn this too. When she learns the joy of being rather than doing and reaches at last the freedom of inner peace and quiet mind, we are right there with her.

Whether you wish to learn about Buddhist meditation or read a love story or learn how to come back from life-threatening depression and anxiety matters not. You will have a peace and understanding of yourself you didn't have before reading *Choosing to Be: Lessons in Living from a Feline Zen Master.*

So read on and allow yourself to be enchanted, mystified, and enthralled.

Patricia Heller
Author of *If You Hear the Message Three Times, Listen*

For a myriad of reasons not really pertinent to this story,
I descended from my executive office on the top floor
of a sleek and stylish high-rise tower
into the underworld of depression in 1993.

I had been there before.

I suppose you could say I was a frequent visitor,
but I usually stopped at one of the upper floors.

This time I took the express elevator—
straight to the basement, the suicide floor.

And wouldn't you know, this particular elevator
required a special key to come back up.

This is the story of how I found the key.

Kat Tansey

Ordinary Mind

So where exactly is this
Buddha nature?
It is in the sky-like nature
of our mind.

—SOGYAL RINPOCHE
The Tibetan Book of Living and Dying

CHAPTER ONE

Deciding to Stay

POOHBEAR DEGOONACOON, my grandly large Maine Coon cat, was stretched across the back of my cozy blue couch, sleeping comfortably next to my shoulder. Awakened by a sudden crash of blowing rain against the skylight, he opened his eyes for a moment, extended his long front paws, yawned, and went back to sleep.

I, too, was startled by the sound. The rain had been a steady presence in the background all morning, but now the wind had picked up and the storm was becoming more forceful. This escalation of the weather suited my mood. For months I had been torn between continuing to exist in my debilitating state of depression on the one hand and the increasingly compelling thought that I should take action and end my life on the other.

All morning, I'd drifted aimlessly around the large, open loft dwelling I shared with my husband Michael, until the orange binding and gold lettering on the spine of a book I'd tucked away on my bookshelf caught my eye. I became deeply engrossed in *The Tibetan Book of Living and Dying* for several hours, reading the first few chapters that dealt with the ever-changing nature of the mind. According to the author, Sogyal Rinpoche, the mind is much like a flea, hopping to and fro from one thought to the next, rarely pausing to reflect and learn from its wanderings.

This gave me pause. While my decision to end my depression by ending my life seemed quite logical, should I trust that my mind was making sense? I stopped to consider my mind as it behaved like a flea, watching as it flitted randomly from thought to thought. If my mind was no more reliable than a flea, then to rely on this same mind to make a wise decision about something as irreversible as death seemed like not such a good idea after all.

I read on. Perhaps I needed to reconsider the notion that I had only two choices. I came upon a passage describing the difference between our *ordinary mind*—the mind I had observed hopping to and fro—and our *Buddha nature*, the sky-like nature of our mind, which is open and limitless and the birthright of every living being.

Intrigued by this idea, I decided I needed to discuss this at length with someone wiser than myself. I looked over at Poohbear, who was still sleeping soundly next to my shoulder. Pooh and I had a long history of dialoguing, and I had learned much from the words of wisdom that came from his bewhiskered cat mouth. I gave him a nudge to wake him up. Slowly, he opened one eye.

"I do hope you have a good reason for disturbing my lovely nap," he grumbled.

I held the book up to show him the page I was reading. "Why do you suppose I picked up this book this morning, Pooh? What do you know about this idea that everyone has a Buddha nature?"

Poohbear opened his eyes more fully and looked at the page. He pulled in his outstretched paws to prop himself up and considered my question.

"Well, until this moment I thought all beings knew about Buddha nature," he replied with a slight yawn. "Cats pass this knowledge down from generation to generation. As a matter of fact, my own mother taught me exactly what it says right there. One does not *become* a Buddha—one simply ceases to be deluded about the nature of one's own mind."

I was stunned. Had I been living with a teacher of Buddhism all this time and didn't even know it? Certainly I knew Pooh was a wise being, and I had consulted with him more than once during our four-year relationship. But this was a surprise.

"Pooh," I replied. "Why haven't you ever brought this up before? Didn't you realize it might be of some help to me?"

Pooh considered this for a moment. "I never thought about it. As I said, I thought all beings knew about Buddha nature. Besides, it is not something one has to think about. It just is," he said with a shrug.

"Well, maybe it *just is* for you, but it sure *just isn't* for me," I replied, now a bit impatient. "No one ever passed this down in my family. The only thing I remember from Sunday school is singing, "Yes, Jesus loves me." The idea that I might already *be* the answer I am seeking is revolutionary to me, to say the least." I put the book down and turned to face him more directly.

"This is not a revolutionary idea, Kat," Pooh said. "It is over 2600 years old. If this is the first you have heard of it, I am beginning to understand why you have been so depressed. Perhaps it is time for me to teach you how to discover your Buddha nature."

I stared at him. "Do you really think this could be my answer, this Buddha nature business? If it has been here all along, why have I struggled so much of my life with depression? Why am I even considering suicide as a choice?"

"You are thinking this way because you are stuck in ordinary mind. It is this ignorance that deludes your thinking and clouds your comprehension of what is real. You can be quite clever, Kat, but there is an old Tibetan saying, "If you are too clever, you miss the point entirely.""

"I'm not feeling clever at all, Pooh. I am utterly and totally confused, vulnerable, and at the end of my rope," I said.

"Good, confusion is an excellent place to begin. If you are willing to let go of certainty and allow yourself to be confused, I can most assuredly help you find your Buddha nature. After all, I helped you considerably during the years you were ill by coaching you in Aggressive Rest Therapy. And, I might add, that was not a particularly easy task given your prior proclivity for action."

I thought about how difficult it had been for me to accept the need for constant rest when I was sick with chronic fatigue. My answer to any problem had always been to take action. The fact that the only action I could take was to rest had been completely foreign to me. After all, hadn't that "proclivity for action" Pooh mentioned been the reason for my successful career?

"It's true you were of significant help during my long illness, Pooh. No one is more of an expert in Aggressive Rest Therapy than you, and I do appreciate that you forced me to learn how to rest. But this matter of finding my Buddha nature—this seems to be a little more esoteric than learning how to lie around and do nothing."

Pooh sat very straight, pulling himself up to his full height, so that he was looking down at me from the back of the couch.

"First of all, Kat, you underrate being able to lie around and do nothing. Few humans do this well, though you were able to make good progress under my tutelage.

"Now, as to this matter of Buddha nature," he continued, "we are talking about you learning to understand the nature of your own mind. Whether you are a human or a cat, the same technique applies. You must learn to sit and meditate. And I happen to know more than a little bit about this," he observed, making a point of sitting back down and tucking both paws under his chest in his best Buddha pose.

I got up and began pacing. Living in a large loft space has several advantages, one of them being plenty of pacing room. My teak desk and large white worktable were situated on an Oriental rug in the center of my big sitting area, allowing me to walk completely around them. I circled them several times, my hands clasped behind my back, thinking about what Pooh had said.

"I would like to believe you, Pooh, but I've tried many times to meditate and never got very far. Why should it be any different now?" I stopped pacing and looked at him, hoping he would have an answer that made sense.

"What does it matter whether it is different now, Kat? You have been struggling with this depression for a long time, and as you have said yourself, you are at the end of your rope. You must trust that you picked up this book this morning for a reason. It is a sign. You need to open yourself up to answers you cannot even envision yet."

He paused for effect and gave me one of his wise, omniscient looks. "I know more about Buddha nature than you can imagine. I can help you. It is only a matter of deciding where to begin."

Pooh stood up and stretched, extending his front legs, then leaning forward and extending his back legs. "I am going to ponder this a bit. You seem like you could do with a cup of tea. Make yourself a nice pot with some cookies, and while you are at it, please put out a little snack for me." With that, he walked across the couch and leaped to the floor, heading around the corner to the kitchen.

I followed him and put the kettle on. He was right. Taking a break with a cup of hot tea was a good idea. While the water was boiling, I put some treats into Pooh's bowl and watched him inhale them. I selected Earl Grey tea from the cupboard. When the kettle whistled, I poured the hot water into the ceramic teapot and took it, along with my favorite cup and a small plate of oatmeal cookies, over to the table. While I was waiting for the tea to brew, Pooh leaped up on the table, licked his paw, and began washing his face.

I watched him wipe his face repeatedly with his paw, marveling at the deep brown tabby markings on his forehead. The small patch of white fur outlining the area around his mouth and chin set them off against his magnificent dark ruff, that long, lush collar of fur that made him look like a lion. How could I possibly doubt any idea suggested by such a regal being? I poured my tea and resumed our conversation.

"Don't get me wrong, Pooh. I'm grateful that you want to help me, and it certainly isn't that I doubt your ability, but I feel like I've been there; I've tried meditation before. I just don't know if I have enough energy left to try yet another approach. I am exhausted from pushing myself every day to survive this unrelenting depression. I don't think I have the strength to try something new."

Poohbear stopped washing his face. "I am aware of how discouraging these four years have been for you, Kat. It was a cruel twist of fate that you were struck with this chronic fatigue shortly after you moved into your new offices, just as you were getting ready to go on your big book tour. I know that to go from all that excitement to lying on a couch for years was quite a challenge for you."

"It isn't just that, Pooh," I replied. "It's that no one knew what was wrong with me, so everyone thought, and some still do, that it was all in my head. At the time, no one knew about the effects of the formaldehyde outgassing from those new cabinets and carpet glue, so I was completely alone in my search for answers about what had happened to me." Just thinking about those years of struggle made me feel so tired I began to cry. I pulled a tissue out of my pocket and wiped my eyes and then tried to drink my tea, but I was too choked up to swallow. I felt as though a lump the size of an apple was in my throat.

Pooh waited for me to compose myself. "I really do know what a struggle this has been for you. And I know that only your own determination and sheer will helped you persevere to find the answers you needed to get well."

I acknowledged what Pooh had said and tried to smile. He did understand. He had been there with me the whole time I was sick. Now that I thought about it, I really hadn't been so alone, had I? Starting to feel a little better, I sipped my tea.

Pooh continued. "Kat, this time you will not have to do this through your own sheer will. You have the opportunity now to learn another way of healing and a very different way of viewing the world. While I was eating, I had an idea. I know how we should begin."

"While you were *wolfing* you mean," I joked. My sense of humor had returned. I guessed I was feeling better.

"Funny. Do you want to hear my idea or not?"

"Sorry, Pooh." I grinned sheepishly. "Of course I want to hear your idea."

"It occurred to me that I was more in touch with the essence of my Buddha nature when I was younger," he said. "We should get a kitten."

"*That's* your solution, Pooh? *A kitten?*"

"It is not the whole solution, Kat. It is just the beginning. Getting a kitten will shake things up. We could use some new life around here, one who looks at everything with the awe of seeing it for the first time. Now, you must look for a kitten who truly knows his Buddha nature. One who just, well, one who just *is*."

I looked at Pooh in amazement. "Did you know I took a photograph of you when you were a little kitten that I used to show to everyone, and we all laughed about how much *you* looked like a little Buddha?"

As I thought about how innocent Poohbear looked in that picture, I suddenly remembered a line from my one of my favorite poems: "Trailing clouds of glory do we come from God, who is our home." William Wordsworth believed heaven surrounds us when we are infants, but as we grow up, "shades of the prison-house begin to close." *Just the way our ordinary mind obscures our Buddha mind—just like Pooh's mother told him. Perhaps Pooh really might know how to help me.*

I imagined what it would be like to have a kitten racing around the loft. Poohbear was almost four years old, and it had been a long time since he had raced for anything other than a bird out in the roof garden. Michael and I missed his headlong flights around the loft, chasing after the cloth mice we threw out like baseballs.

I picked up another cookie and thought about how nice it might be to have a younger brother for Pooh. Names were always a big deal for me, so as I was warming up to the idea, I mused about what we would call the kitten. I had a book of cat pictures titled *Zen Cat*. This kitten would be Poohbear's younger brother—so something with Zen and bear in the name would be perfect.

"You may be right, Pooh. Getting a kitten might be a good way for us to learn about Buddha nature." And then the name came to me. "We could call him Catzenbear." I looked over at Poohbear for his approval.

"I am glad to see you are becoming enthused about the idea,

but you have missed the point. While I did say a kitten might be more in touch with his Buddha nature, he will hardly have the wisdom to teach *us* about it."

"Oh yes, of course, Pooh, you are absolutely right," I replied, backpedaling delicately. "A kitten couldn't possibly possess your understanding and wisdom."

"Correct. A kitten may be closer to his essence, but remember, kittens have a lot to learn," Pooh said. "Wisdom only comes with experience and study."

"I understand," I said cautiously. "Thank you for clarifying the difference between the Buddha nature of a kitten and the wisdom you possess, Pooh."

I got up to put my dishes in the sink and picked up my phone book from the counter to look up Pooh's breeder. "I'll give Alex a call. I don't know if she will have any kittens available right now, but we won't know until I ask her."

All sentient beings have
Buddha nature.

–THE BUDDHA
Mahaparinirvana Sutra

CHAPTER TWO

Building the Team

ALEX RETURNED MY CALL the next morning, and I was delighted to hear she had a litter of five-week-old kittens. The mother of the litter was Tikka, who was Poohbear's mother, and the father was Jeremy, Pooh's grandfather. *Well, they certainly have the right lineage.* I smiled as I realized how seriously I was taking this search for a kitten who, as Pooh had instructed, "Truly knows his Buddha nature." You would think I was looking for the Dalai Lama himself.

Alex said she had promised all five kittens to buyers, but another of her mother cats was ready to deliver, so she could put off one of the buyers if we found Catzenbear in this litter. "You know, Kat," she said, "there is one kitten who seems to have quite a special sense of himself. Come tomorrow and see him." I smiled again—now Alex was engaged in the quest for the enlightened being.

That night after dinner, I approached my husband Michael about getting a kitten. His concern, rightly enough, was the cost. Maine Coon cats were expensive. The only reason we purchased Poohbear rather than finding a kitten at the Humane Society was because of Michael's allergies to every cat but Maine Coons. Even though Alex offered to sell me a kitten at the same price we'd paid for Poohbear almost four years ago, it was still a lot of money. But we needed this kitten, and somehow Michael understood this. He was frustrated that there was nothing he could do to help me find my way out of this depression, and he hoped perhaps a new life in the form of a kitten would help.

"We'll find the money," he said.

The next day, I made the long drive from our loft building in downtown Los Angeles to Alex's house in Northridge. This was the first time in more than a month I'd ventured outside other than my weekly trips to Pasadena to see my therapist, who was valiantly trying to help me pull out of my downward spiral. My long struggle with chronic fatigue had pretty much cut off my contact with friends and associates. It was hard to stay in touch when you couldn't concentrate and became exhausted after a few minutes on the telephone, so eventually everyone had just slipped away, back into their busy lives.

Then my mother was diagnosed with Alzheimer's disease and I hit menopause full-on at the same time. So, just as I was brought face-to-face with something I thought I had accepted long ago—the fact that I was never going to have a child—I was losing my mom. The links on both sides of me were being severed, and I kept having dreams in which I was floating away.

But today I was on a mission to find this kitten named Catzenbear. I showered and put on some nice slacks and a dark sweater instead of my usual sweat clothes. I even fixed my hair and put on some makeup. I didn't look like the stylish executive in high heels and designer suit I had been in my former life, but at least I could pass for someone who was a few loops up from the bottom of the depression spiral.

It was wonderful to see Alex again. She had bushy blond hair, a husky voice, and enough energy for three people—and she was absolutely passionate about her Maine Coon cats. Michael and I had to go through an extensive interview before she would let us purchase Poohbear, and we had to sign a contract stating that we would meet her stringent requirements for his care.

She greeted me with her usual warmth and enthusiasm,

and took me immediately to the bedroom where Tikka and her litter of five tiny kittens were sequestered. Seeing those five little bundles of fur nestled up to Tikka made me feel happier than I'd felt in weeks.

One of the kittens noticed we were there and walked toward us with his eyes clear and focused and his tail straight up. He came forward with absolute confidence that we were there to receive him with open arms. His ears were alert, with small tufts at the top, and his four bright-white paws made his feet seem too big for the rest of his body. He had white circles around his green-gold eyes that made them seem even larger than they were.

In my readings about Buddhism, I had learned that the holy men, called Brahmins, told the Buddha's father his child would be special. After the Buddha was born, they examined the baby looking for signs of that specialness. The book listed specific traits including long ear lobes, long arms, and long, tapered fingers. *Here I go again. I am taking this Buddha nature thing much too seriously.*

I watched closely as the kitten approached and could see he was, indeed, special. The other kittens were now tumbling over one another, involved in their own activities, not the least interested in meditative pursuits. Only this one came over with an air of knowing where he belonged. Alex smiled at me. "I think you've found Catzenbear."

I sat very still. Catzenbear approached and tried to climb up on my knee, which proved too high for him. He walked around my legs looking for a way up. After trying several approaches, all proving too difficult, he came back to his original position and sat looking up at me. I leaned forward and picked him up. His tiny body fit easily in the palm of my hand.

He looked into my eyes, uttered a small mew, and blinked.

He sat very still in my hand as we touched noses. I put him on my lap, where he curled up and immediately fell asleep. I turned to Alex, "You're right, this is definitely Catzenbear."

Six weeks later, Catzenbear came to live with us. I was so excited the day we brought him home. I had been telling Pooh how special Catzenbear was, so I was brimming with anticipation of Poohbear's loving reception.

Catzenbear trotted over with his attitude of complete confidence, just as he had with me—and Pooh hissed at him. Then Catzenbear wandered off to investigate something else. When he approached Pooh again, he was just as assured and enthusiastic as he had been before. Pooh hissed at him again.

I took Poohbear into the other room. "I don't understand, Pooh. It was your idea to get Catzenbear in the first place. Why on earth are you being so hostile?"

"You are reading more into my actions than you should," Pooh replied. "It is appropriate for me to establish order. I must teach Catzenbear that I am the Master. Otherwise, he will be confused."

"You expect me to believe that Catzenbear welcomes being treated so rudely?"

"Well, this is your perception based on your Southern upbringing and beliefs about good manners and hospitality. You must remember, Kat, yours is only one view of how the world should be. It is not the only view."

Pooh was enjoying his role as a teacher a little too much, I thought.

"Watch Catzenbear's actions closely," he continued. "What you interpret as hostility or rejection from me does not have that effect on him at all. He simply goes off to investigate some other part of his new home, only to return to me later, as if nothing happened, and begin again with his inappropriate behavior. He will repeat this process many times. Eventually, he will learn to temper his enthusiasm when approaching me, and I will begin to respond to him with more warmth. This is a process we go though to learn how to act with one another, to learn who is boss. Catzenbear does not take it personally. He is just being himself."

"In other words," I said slowly, "Catzenbear just *is*."

"Now you are catching on," replied Pooh, as he stretched out on the rug to take a little nap.

Just remain on your
cushion without expecting
anything. Then eventually
you will resume your own
true nature.

—SHUNRYU SUZUKI
Zen Mind, Beginner's Mind

CHAPTER THREE
Just Sitting

DURING THE WEEKS we were waiting to bring Catzenbear home, I investigated meditation centers in the Los Angeles area. One day I saw a small listing in the paper about an introductory lecture on Buddhism sponsored by a local adult learning group. Now that I'd found Catzenbear, I was feeling a little more optimistic about being able to overcome my depression, and I had begun making brief forays into the outside world. I talked to Poohbear about the upcoming lecture.

"I don't know, Pooh. This is only a four-hour introduction to Buddhism. It probably doesn't cover any more than I've read in my books."

"That may be true, Kat, but the teacher might be able to tell you about places where you can learn more. I am happy to help as much as I can, but after all, you are a different species, and I can only do so much. You will also require a human teacher."

I knew he was right. I had avoided telling my therapist about my reliance on my talks with Poohbear, sensing this might be cause for concern on her part. If I was serious about pulling out of this depression, I would eventually have to talk to other humans. Well, I needed to start somewhere. This might well be the place to begin.

The lecture was being held at a hotel in Culver City where I had often taught management seminars in what now seemed like another lifetime. As I walked through the lobby, I saw my reflection in the mirrored wall and was stunned at the contrast between the memory of myself as an attractive, self-confident woman with streaked blond hair, clicking along in high heels and an expensive suit, and the reflection of this rather plain, brown-haired woman in a dark sweater and pants. How in the world did I get from there to here?

I found the lecture room and took a seat in the back. The teacher was a woman named Leonarda who lived at a Buddhist meditation center. She told us she had been practicing meditation for five years, and explained that the type of meditation she practiced, called Insight Meditation, helped one develop concentrated awareness and gain insight into the changing nature of the mind. She went on to tell us the story of the Buddha and his basic teachings. Then she led us through a guided meditation, in which she first helped us focus on our breathing and then took us on an imaginary walk in a beautiful garden. As she described the garden in detail, she would frequently remind us to continue our awareness of breathing in and breathing out or, as she called it, our "in breath" and our "out breath."

The combination of her guided visualization and breathing instruction was quite powerful. I found myself becoming more centered, and I was even able to let go of my constant mind chatter. What a relief to have a quiet mind, if only for a brief time.

After the class, I stayed behind to talk to Leonarda about the meditation center where she lived. She said it was in Koreatown, a community just west of downtown Los Angeles, and invited me to attend the talk at the center that coming Sunday.

I went that Sunday and continued to attend the Sunday talks for many weeks. The center was a pale yellow cottage-style house in a residential neighborhood, but once I entered, I was in another world filled with cushions on the floor, incense in the air, and Buddhist art on the walls. I'd arrive each Sunday and sit meditating for a while with the other meditators. Then I would listen intently to the speaker and stay afterward for tea. I probably spoke only a few dozen words during those first weekly visits, but the people at the center didn't seem bothered by my silent presence.

I heard one of the speakers talk about the three jewels of Buddhist practice: the Buddha, the dharma (the teachings), and the sangha. The sangha was the term for the group who sat in meditation and pursued the practice of Buddhism together. I was beginning to feel comfortable just being in this sangha among the other meditators, but I was still feeling too withdrawn to communicate with them.

It didn't matter, though, because while I didn't feel up to asking the teachers or other students about the mechanics of sitting meditation, I was able to come home and discuss it with Poohbear. We had our own sangha.

One Sunday when I arrived home from the Center, I sought Pooh out to get his advice about the best posture for sitting. I found him upstairs on the bed, looking out at the garden. Our bedroom had a large sliding glass door that provided a view of our garden as well as the skyline of downtown Los Angeles beyond it. At night we could see the lights of the skyscrapers, and in the daytime we could see the flowers.

I joined Pooh on the bed and presented him with my dilemma. "The problem is, Pooh, I don't think I'm doing this right. I'm trying to follow the instructions on how to sit that I found in *Zen Mind, Beginner's Mind*. The author makes it seem very important to sit in a specific position, but I have so much trouble doing this. I find I'm preoccupied with whether I am sitting properly and maintaining the right posture. And then when I try to concentrate on my breathing, being aware of the in breath and the out breath, I start feeling even more anxious."

Pooh listened quietly. He sat quite still for what seemed like a long time. I finally stopped waiting for a reply and just sat beside him.

"Well," he said finally, "it may be that you cannot learn how to sit by reading a book or having someone tell you how to do it. Perhaps you need to be shown. Just sit with me for a while and see what happens."

I thought about how envious I was of his ability to sit for hours without moving, and realized that instead of envying him, perhaps I could try to emulate him.

"Okay, let's give it a try. Should I sit in any particular position?" I asked.

"Just find a way to sit that you can maintain comfortably for some time. Move around until you think you have the posture that works for you. You will know it when you find it." Pooh jumped down to the floor, turned three circles, and settled with his paws tucked under him.

I took a large pillow from the bed and joined him on the floor. First I tried the lotus position that I'd been trying in vain to perfect at the meditation center, but I never was able to keep my feet positioned up on my thighs, and my legs kept going to sleep. I tried other positions to no avail. Finally I tried putting my legs under me in a kneeling position. This felt better but I knew I wouldn't be able to maintain it very long without cutting off the circulation in my legs.

I looked over at Pooh. He was sitting quietly with his front legs tucked under his chest. How could I tuck my legs under me without losing feeling? I tried sitting on the pillow with my legs tucked back on each side of it. It didn't provide quite enough height. I pulled another pillow down from the bed. That still wasn't high enough, so I folded it in half and placed it on top of the bottom pillow.

And that was it. It felt wonderful. I squirmed around until everything settled into place, and I felt grounded and secure. Then I let my arms hang down and folded my hands. At first I tried to make a perfect circle with my fingers and thumbs, but I became distracted trying to figure out if it was perfect enough, so I just let my hands find their own position.

I took a deep breath and relaxed my spine.

I looked over at Poohbear. He was still sitting quietly. He seemed so tranquil, as though he could sit there forever. Watching him, I began to feel some tranquility myself. I closed my eyes and just sat.

I remembered a chapter in Shunryu Suzuki's book *Zen Mind, Beginners Mind* titled "Mind Waves," and an image of waves allowed me to let my thoughts roll in and out like the tide, without becoming attached to them.

Pooh and I sat like this for some time. Nothing special. No extraordinary breakthroughs or spectacular visual effects. We just sat.

I was quite pleased with myself. I had managed to sit for almost an hour without physical discomfort, so I expected that my next sitting would be even better now that I had found a position that worked for me.

The next day was Sunday, and I went to the center to hear another teacher speak. I arrived an hour early to meditate and settled into my new position. But then I became worried about whether I really looked like a meditator. Everyone else sitting in the circle looked so perfect in his or her lotus position. Next I became so preoccupied with following my breath that I had trouble breathing at all. I struggled to last the hour and was exhausted when the bell sounded.

I was very discouraged. Normally the teacher spoke for an hour. I wasn't sure I could take sitting there for another hour feeling so inadequate, but I decided to at least listen for a while. After all, my main purpose for coming to the center every week was to find a teacher with whom I could feel comfortable.

And then Jason Siff, a teacher I had not heard before, began to speak. He began by saying his talk wouldn't last the hour. *He must be reading my mind.* I smiled inwardly. He was younger than the other teachers, but there was something about his caring, quiet manner that made me feel comfortable. He said he wanted to share some of his experiences with meditation and then he wanted to hear about ours.

He talked about how difficult it was for a new meditator to follow the breath. "The breath is moving," he said, "and following something that moves can lead to agitation. It might be easier for you to focus on the still points of contact with your body, such as the touch of your hands on your legs or the touch of your buttocks on the cushion."

My tension dissolved as I listened to him. He *was* reading my mind. He spoke honestly about what he had learned and was still learning in his own practice. He was very approachable and encouraged us to talk about our experiences.

Fortunately, some of the other students asked many of the same questions I had. While it seemed to me that they knew exactly what they were doing and how to do it, it turned out they, too, were struggling with comparisons and doubts about whether they were sitting properly or breathing correctly.

What a revelation! I wanted to laugh out loud at myself and my assumptions. So, I wasn't the only one having trouble learning this. After hearing some of the other students' questions, I felt comfortable enough to share how difficult it was to sit with my self-critical thoughts and ask for guidance.

Jason suggested I let my thoughts come and go and begin to observe them, then reflect back on them after they had passed. He emphasized *gently* returning the mind to the still points of the body, such as our hands on our laps or the touch of our buttocks, or in my case knees, on the cushion, rather than following the movement of the breath.

I began to understand. If I could gently return my attention to the still points, I would become more grounded and could let go of my incessant mind chatter. I had been able to do this successfully when I sat at home with Pooh, but in the glare of being in the "perfect meditator" spotlight at the center, I lost my ability to ground myself. *Using the still points will be a big help, no matter where I sit. And gently returning my attention to the still points—what a concept!* The key word here was *gently*. My approach was to force and punish my mind. Adopting this new gentle approach would require some practice.

After the discussion, I introduced myself to Jason and his wife Jacquelin and learned Jason had been a Buddhist monk in Sri Lanka, and Jacquelin a Theravada Buddhist nun in Asia. They were both Americans, and after three years they had decided to come back to the United States to teach meditation, giving up their robes and shaved heads and returning to their married state and former attire. Jason had a full head of very curly hair, and Jacquelin had beautiful long black hair. Dressed as they were in casual Western clothes, it was hard for me to imagine them looking like the other monks and nuns that came to the center.

Jacquelin and I got a cup of tea, and she asked me how it was that I had come to the Community Meditation Center. It was clear that I was not part of the group there, since I hadn't talked to anyone else during the social time and had just stood waiting to talk to Jason. As soon as she asked me that, the floodgates opened and I started telling her how weighted down by loneliness I was. I explained that I had been ill for a long time and that trying to participate in conversations was still quite exhausting, so I was stuck in my own head most of the time. She saw how much pain I was in and told me I was much closer than I thought to being able to meditate. Her words of encouragement made me cry. Jacquelin acted as if this display of emotion was perfectly normal and gave me a gentle hug.

I had found my teachers.

When I came home, Poohbear was on the couch trying to nap, exhausted from dealing with Catzenbear's antics, which Pooh said had involved putting several large pieces of fragile sculpture at risk. I told him what had happened at the meditation center. He said he was pleased I had found humans who would reinforce the lessons he was teaching me, but he was just too tired from babysitting Catz to hear more. I gave him a hug and went to see what mischief Catzenbear was up to.

Joy isn't something
we have to find. Joy
is who we are if we're
not preoccupied with
something else.

—CHARLOTTE JOKO BECK
Nothing Special

CHAPTER FOUR
Finding Joy

WHAT HAPPENED NEXT surprised me. Everything in my life was moving forward at a steady pace. I'd found my teachers. Pooh and I were unraveling the mysteries of meditation. Michael was pleased that I seemed to be feeling better and was getting out more. And me? I couldn't stop crying.

One of my favorite literary wits, Dorothy Parker, was known for her exclamation, "What fresh hell is this?" I kept asking myself that question as I wandered around our loft, often on the verge of tears. I pretended to be okay when Michael was there, but as soon as he left I'd fall into long spells of walking and weeping.

One day Michael came up to the loft unexpectedly in the middle of the day. I was pacing around crying uncontrollably when he walked in and caught me by surprise. I felt trapped. I didn't want him to see me like that.

"Why did you come up here without calling first?" I asked.

He was taken aback by my question and my tears. He asked what was wrong, but since I didn't know what was wrong, I just said I needed time to be by myself and wished he would let me know when he was coming upstairs.

I must have hit a nerve, because he responded by telling me that this was his home, too, and he should be able to come up whenever he wished, and things went quickly downhill from there.

"For God's sake, Michael, you have your office and your studio downstairs. There is nowhere here I can be alone," I shouted.

Michael just turned around and stormed out. The heavy door slammed behind him with a loud thud.

I threw myself down on the couch in the living room area and cried even more. Finally, I calmed down. I got up and went around the corner to my writing room, an area separated by two eight-foot walls that didn't reach to the twenty-foot loft ceiling. The walls kept my office and sitting room out of sight, but they provided no real solitude for me. There was no completely private place to hide out in our loft, other than the bathroom.

Pooh was resting on the blue couch in my office. He had wisely decided not to get anywhere near the fracas on the other side of the wall. I sat down next to him, exhausted.

"What is wrong with me, Pooh? I'm falling apart. And now I've attacked Michael when he's been doing everything he can to help."

"Well, there is no denying you are a bit of a mess today, Kat—as you have been for the past few days. Perhaps it was easier for you to cope when you were hoping you were not going to be around much longer," Pooh said gently.

"I don't understand, Pooh. I felt so depressed and hopeless before—I didn't see how I could go on. At least now I'm starting to get back into life. Wouldn't you think I would feel better?"

"You do feel better, Kat, and that is exactly why you are in such a state. The impact of what is going on in your life is starting to sink in."

And then it hit me. The discussions with Dad and his rage at losing Mom to Alzheimer's. Mom asking me, "So, where are you living now, honey?" ten times during a five-minute conversation. My menopausal hot flashes and sleepless nights getting up to change my nightgown and sit in front of a fan.

"Oh my God, Pooh, you're right. Before, I was so depressed

I was too numb to feel anything. Now it's all flooding in. How heartbroken I am not being able to really connect with Mom any longer. How angry I am at the way Dad treats her like a child and refuses to get any help. How frustrated I am because just as I was getting my health back, my hormones and sleeplessness are zapping my energy. And I'm feeling tremendous pressure to pretend to Michael that I'm making progress, so he won't feel we have wasted money by continuing with my therapy and getting Catzenbear."

"Yes, Kat. You are waking up and becoming aware. You are feeling again. No more numbness," Pooh said.

"No wonder I can't stop crying." I took a deep breath, letting this realization wash over me.

Pooh sat quietly. Then he said, "Do you remember when I jumped into that open skylight, and it turned out the ceiling I thought I was going to land on was made of paper, and I fell twenty feet into the neighbor's loft?"

Our private roof garden had a small opening to the roof of our block-long loft building. Michael had designed it that way so he could provide access to his crew when they needed to make repairs. Pooh had figured out how to get through the opening and often spent his days exploring various parts of the building's roof. Since all the third-floor lofts in the building had skylights, he was able to look in on our neighbors when their skylights were open. One day he had decided to visit one of our neighbors by jumping through their open skylight, landing on a ceiling made only of paper, which of course could not withstand the weight of a twenty-pound cat.

"Of course I remember that, Pooh. It took us all day to figure out where you were, since our neighbors were out of town. You were not in excellent shape when we found you."

"True. But I *did* have time to be alone and lick my wounds," Pooh said knowingly. "You do not."

I looked at him and thought about the significance of what he'd said.

Just then Catzenbear bounced in. He tried to get up on the couch but couldn't, and fell in a heap on the rug. He immediately got up and tried again with the same result. And again, and again.

I laughed at how determined he was and then picked him up and put him on my lap. He immediately jumped off to go over and bat at Pooh. Pooh gave him a small hiss, and Catzenbear curled up next to him to go to sleep.

"Catz is so adorable, Pooh. He's such a little clown, isn't he?"

"Catzenbear does whatever comes into his mind, with no self-consciousness to get in the way. You do realize, Kat, that his antics just helped shift your mood. Do you feel the difference?"

"I do. So what are you saying? If I allow myself to let in my feelings of grief and anger, I can also begin to experience joy?" I reached over and picked up Catzenbear and kissed him on his nose. Then I put him back next to Pooh.

"That is exactly what I am saying, Kat," Pooh replied, as he allowed Catzenbear to snuggle in next to him again.

Later that evening I apologized to Michael. I was honest with him about my hiding out so I wouldn't disappoint him. I told him I was trying to act like I was feeling better, because my definition of feeling better didn't include fits of crying and I didn't want him to worry.

Michael gave me a hug and told me how much he loved me and that he appreciated my honesty. He said he wanted to go fly-fishing and suggested we get away for a few days, thinking the change of scenery might be good for us. He looked down at Catz and Pooh and said it would be easy to take them along.

The next week we all drove up to the cabin we occasionally rented in Hot Creek. The weather was perfect in the mountains, just warm enough to enjoy being outside. When Michael set off every morning to fish, I'd walk along with him down the winding path through the grassy meadow to the river. Sometimes I'd stay down there for a while, watching the water surge and swirl around the rocks and fallen logs before going back up to the cabin.

At our loft in Los Angeles, I'd been taking photographs using high-speed black-and-white film to try to capture Catzenbear in action. The loft had great lighting from all the large windows and skylights, but because there was so much open space, it was hard to keep up with him. The cabin here was small so I was able to get within a few feet, and the morning light was perfect. I threw Catz a toy mouse to play with on the couch and started shooting. Later, when I developed the film, I saw I had captured him in a back flip. What a picture of absolute, unabashed joy! Every time I look at it, I get a big grin on my face.

Pooh was sitting on the chair near the couch, where he had been watching my photography efforts with half-closed eyes. Catzenbear became bored with the toy mouse and went off to explore other parts of the cabin, so this seemed like a good time to meditate. I got my meditation cushion, settled in, and when I found my place—that spot where my body felt most comfortably propped on the cushion—I closed my eyes and watched my thoughts. How happy and content I was in this moment. Then the thought that we would be going back downtown in a few days came up like a big thundercloud, and I started feeling sad. Next my mind went to the thought that neither of my parents had been able to visit us in the loft, and now it was too late for Mom to come. Then I wondered if Michael had caught any fish for dinner. I kept coming back to my breathing and the still point of my hands in my lap as I watched all the thoughts, happy and sad, and let them pass.

And so it went, with Pooh sitting right beside me. When I opened my eyes and looked at the clock, I was surprised to find that more than an hour had passed. I picked up my journal and went outside to write down what I remembered of my meditation, leaving the two cats asleep in the chair.

Late in the afternoon, I went off to find Michael. Wanting a high vantage point from which to look for him, I followed the path up to the rocky cliff that overlooked the entire meadow. The tall grass was gently bending and blowing in the warm breeze, and the beauty of the deep blue river meandering through the soft golden grass made me wish I'd brought my camera. The sun was going down, turning everything a soft amber color, and the swallows began swooping around the cliff, darting after insects that must have thought the end of the day a safe time to come out. Michael saw me and waved, and we both started back.

We met at the bend in the river and walked together while he talked about his day. This was a catch-and-release river, but you could keep enough fish for your own dinner, and Michael proudly showed me the three good-sized trout he'd kept. *Plenty of fish for all four of us,* I thought with a smile.

We got to the cabin just as it was getting dark and a little chilly, so I went into the bedroom to put on a sweater. Pooh was on the bed. I gave him a hug and told him how much joy I had felt watching the swallows do their daredevil acts off the cliffs. Catzenbear came in and tried to get on the bed and couldn't, so I picked him up and left him with Pooh while I went to help Michael prepare our dinner.

That night, I decided to read Charlotte Beck's *Everyday Zen* to see whether she had written anything about joy in that book, as she had in another of her books I'd read several weeks before. It was on the first page: "My dog doesn't worry about the meaning of life. She may worry if she doesn't get breakfast, but she doesn't sit around worrying about whether she will get fulfilled or liberated or enlightened." What a joyful state of being.

I looked over at Michael, asleep on the couch with Catzenbear sprawled on his chest, and had to laugh at how fulfilled, liberated, and enlightened they both seemed. I turned to Pooh and told him I was beginning to understand how important the ability to feel joy was to my meditation practice.

"I am glad you see this, Kat," said Pooh. "Your feeling joy will help you let go of sadness and grief. When you are not trying to avoid feelings or hang on to feelings in meditation, you can just sit and watch them flow by. You begin to understand that all of these feelings are, as Ram Dass said, 'grist for the mill.'"

"*Hmmm,* I didn't know you were familiar with Ram Dass, Pooh."

Pooh stood up and stretched. "There is a lot you do not know about me, Kat," he said as he leaped to the floor and headed for the kitchen. "Now that you are paying attention, you will begin to see what has been right before your eyes all this time."

Walk as if you are kissing
the earth with your feet.

–THICH NHAT HANH
Peace Is Every Step

CHAPTER FIVE

Walking on Our Toes

I WAS LOOKING FORWARD to sitting with my meditation group the Sunday after we returned from Hot Creek. We met at Gordon Smith's house in Mount Washington, an area just north of downtown Los Angeles. Gordon shared his love for Buddhism and meditation by inviting us into his home on Tuesday nights and Sunday afternoons.

His home was simple and sparsely furnished in a 1970s style, with olive-colored couches and a deep red Oriental rug on wood flooring. Authentic Japanese scrolls hung on the dark wood walls, and a large library of Buddhist writings and Japanese art books took up one side of the living room. Large bay windows overlooked a big wooden deck. It was a perfect place for a meditation retreat. Additionally, it was graced by the presence of Gordon's cat, who occasionally would do one of us the great honor of sitting on our lap during meditation.

The house was built on the side of a hill and looked out on a small forest of pine and eucalyptus trees. I would often sit outside on the deck to meditate so I could enjoy the smell of the pines and the breeze gently caressing my face. Our first of three sittings was always short, just twenty minutes, and I was so happy to be back with the group that it was easy for me to let go of my thoughts. My sitting reflected my peaceful, happy state of mind. The bell rang to signify the end of the sitting, and we all went inside for discussion. My life is really blessed, I thought, as I listened to the others describe their meditation experiences to Jason.

It was getting a little cold outside, so we took our wraps out with us for the second sitting. I settled into the chair I liked to use when no one else claimed it first, and felt very pleased that I got it this time. After wrapping my shawl around me, I closed my eyes, relaxed my spine, and looked forward to a deep and profound meditation.

And then I began to squirm. And fidget. I could not keep still. My thoughts were all over the place. The noise of the leaves being swept across the deck by the wind was deafening. The traffic sounds from beyond the trees were like Times Square at rush hour. I felt like ants were crawling on me. My sitting became the longest sitting recorded in the history of mankind.

Finally, the bell rang.

Exhausted and despondent, I went to the kitchen to get a cup of tea. I told Jacquelin how disappointed I was. She smiled and said that when we come to the practice of meditation depressed and in pain, we are often more receptive to sitting because it is easier to be still when we are tired and depressed. Now that I was feeling better, she said, it would be more of a struggle. Learning to sit in the active Western world, with an active Western mind, was not a particularly easy path.

Poohbear was awake when I came home, and I shared my frustration with him. "Gee, Pooh, you'd think getting out of depression would be a good thing. Now here I am not doing well in my meditation group because I can feel again."

"I am not surprised that you are having some trouble," he said. "You should be aware by now that you often have expectations about your sittings. This sitting will be hard, you think. This sitting will be peaceful. This sitting will be—whatever it is you create in your mind."

I went over to sit down beside him on the couch. It felt good to be on my comfortable sofa instead of the hard couches at Gordon's house. "I suppose I do have expectations about my sittings, Pooh, but this was different. I began the sitting with a feeling of well-being, and then I just couldn't sit still. I don't think my mind was causing it. My body wanted action." I told him what Jacquelin said about how it was often difficult sitting in the busyness of the Western world.

"Yes, this makes sense to me," Pooh said with a Buddha-like nod. "I do not have the opportunity to get out much, but I often watch your friends and neighbors down by the pool in the courtyard from our roof garden. They are so agitated, and they talk all the time. I can see how it would be difficult for them to sit and meditate for more than a few seconds, much less minutes. I suspect that since you have more energy now, you are becoming a little more like them. If this is the case, of course you will find it harder to sit. Your body and mind want action."

I moved some of the pillows aside to get more comfortable—now that I wasn't "sitting" I was quite focused on my physical comfort. "I don't expect this path to be easy, Pooh. But every time I make progress I'm beset with new problems—often, it seems, caused by the very progress I am making. I started to feel better, and then all hell broke loose as thoughts and feelings I'd been suppressing came flooding in. Now I'm beginning to have more energy and even a little joy in my life—and my ability to sit seems to have vanished."

Pooh smiled a knowing smile. "All of this is to be expected, Kat. Instead of being disappointed by what you call setbacks, look for the deeper meaning. With each setback, it means you are ready to develop the skill and capacity to take the next step. If you look at these passages as opportunities to take your practice to a new level, you will find a way to move through them. You must be open to new solutions."

Then, having given me the benefit of his wisdom, Pooh tucked his head under his paw to block the light from his eyes and promptly went to sleep, leaving me to reflect on what he had said.

I realized he was right. When I looked back over my progress as a meditator, I could see how each setback led to my next lesson, and then on to further progress. I decided I would try to keep an open mind.

Later that day, Michael and I drove to West Los Angeles to visit his family. On the way back we stopped at a health food store, and I noticed a flyer on the bulletin board for a one-day walking meditation seminar. It was to be held that weekend at a retreat center in the hills above Malibu. I thought about what Pooh had said about keeping an open mind and decided this might be one of the new solutions he had spoken about.

Early Saturday I made the drive to Malibu. It really did feel good to be getting out in the world again. I looked forward to learning another aspect of meditation and appreciated the opportunity to get out of downtown and back into nature.

The setting was incredibly beautiful. The center was an old wooden lodge that had been restored and turned into a retreat house. The meditation room had several large windows that brought the beauty of the forest inside. There were many species of tall trees: eucalyptus, pines, oaks, sycamores, and some I couldn't name. A winding gravel path led to the edge of the mountain and overlooked the Pacific Ocean. I was up so high I imagined that I could almost see the curve of the ocean at the horizon.

There were smaller paths leading to several different gardens, some filled with herbs and others with succulent plants, all with benches and arbors inviting one to rest and reflect.

Our instructions were simple. We were to walk the paths and be aware each time we lifted and placed each foot. If our thoughts wandered, we were to return to the lifting and placing, or to our breathing. We would do this for a set amount of time and then come back to listen to the teacher talk about meditation and discuss our experiences. Then we'd have time to practice walking again and apply what we had learned from the discussion.

I liked having the ability to move while meditating because then I wasn't distracted by any restlessness my body might feel. I was able to pay more attention to watching my thoughts and letting them go. A light breeze cooled the air, and following the gravel paths, I didn't have to think about where I was going. Every now and then I would intersect with another path and see some of my fellow meditators walking as precisely as I was. How comforting it was to be walking the paths with them!

At the end of the day I drove home with renewed confidence and enthusiasm for my meditation practice.

The next morning, I decided to try doing a walking meditation in our loft. Though it was separated into dining, living, and sleeping areas, the loft was so large it still had long open spaces. There was plenty of room to walk without running into anything. I stood, took a few deep breaths to center myself, and began walking, concentrating on lifting and placing my feet just as we had done in Malibu.

All was well and good except for the fact that Catzenbear had not been in Malibu.

He found my new behavior quite interesting. First he followed me. Then he ran ahead of me. And then he pounced. Every time I took a step, he'd jump on my foot. I could clearly see this was not going to work in the peaceful meditative way it had in Malibu. Since locking Catzenbear in the bathroom didn't seem a Buddha-like solution, I decided to go out to the roof garden to practice.

Again I centered and concentrated on lifting and placing my feet. This worked for one walk around the garden, and then it stopped as, surprise, surprise, I became lost in my thoughts. Worries about money. What kind of work could I do to help out financially? Should I work in a bookstore? That probably wouldn't be a good idea because I was still so affected by chemicals and other substances. I had recently spent an hour in a bookstore and found the newly printed material gave me a terrific headache.

Then I realized how lost in thought I was—like when you're driving and suddenly realize you have driven miles without knowing it. Okay. Stop. Center. Start again.

Now I began having trouble keeping my breathing in sync with the lifting and placing. *Breathe in for three steps, out for three steps. Come on, Kat, you can do it,* I thought as I struggled on. Between figuring out how many lift-and-places I had done so I could breathe, and bringing my mind back from whatever distant financial land it was in, I was not having what one might call a peak meditation experience. I decided to call it quits for the day.

Pooh was sleeping on the long beige couch in the living room, so I sat down with a thump, hoping to wake him. I sighed loudly, expecting him to ask me how my practice had gone. He said nothing. I sighed again. Still nothing. I went over to the kitchen and got out the container of cat food, shaking it a little as I poured a small amount into his dish. That did it. He bounded over.

I sipped a drink of water waiting for him to finish, and then we went back to the couch. I explained to him what had happened. "It was so difficult to keep everything in sync while I was practicing the walking meditation, Pooh. I kept losing my place."

Just then Catzenbear hopped up onto the glass-covered dining room table and walked across it. Pooh and I watched, and

Pooh asked me what I saw.

"Well," I said, "Catzenbear is walking. It is a pleasure to watch him move."

"There is more to it than that. You see, cats do not get lost in thought. Catzenbear is an empty vessel. Look, he is walking back the other way now. Just watch what he is doing."

"He is walking on his toes," I said, "and he seems to be placing each paw with intention." I watched his paws and laughed. "He is doing paw-paw-paw-paw. He's aware of the placement of his paws without making it look like work."

"Right. Now go out and do what he is doing. Empty your mind and imitate him."

So I went back out to the roof. Smiling, I closed my eyes and imagined Catzenbear walking. I opened my eyes, took a deep breath, and began.

This time I placed my feet as though they were paws instead of leading with my heels. I tried saying *lift* and *place* each time I lifted and placed my foot, the way I had learned at the seminar. That was too confusing, so I decided to just say *paw* each time I put my foot down.

So there I was in my roof garden, walking and saying *paw-paw-paw-paw*. I breathed in with two paws and out with two paws. After one round, I started breathing more deeply: in with four paws and out with four paws.

I settled into the rhythm of it. And then I started thinking about the bookstore and how I would have enjoyed working there. How hard it was going to be for me to get back out into the world now that I was so affected by perfumes and chemicals. Whoops. *Paw-paw-paw-paw.*

Maybe I could find a writing project or some sort of part-time consulting work. But I no longer had the business contacts to make that happen, and besides, I wasn't sure I could concentrate well enough to take something like that on. *Paw-paw-paw-paw.* Another ripple about money. *Paw-paw-paw-paw.* Anxiety about how I would know when I was really well enough to get back out there without suffering a relapse. *Paw-paw-paw-paw.*

Settle down. Follow my breath and my paws. Just walk. Paw-paw-paw-paw.

When I stopped, I was delighted that I had been able to become aware of my thoughts—to feel emotions coming up, catch them, and let them go. I found Poohbear and told him how well my practice had gone. Then I went to find Catz and gave him a big hug to thank him for helping so much. We went over to the couch to join Pooh, who pointed out it was not really Catzenbear who helped me—Catz was just being himself.

"Of course, Pooh," I said quickly. "And you were wise enough to teach me how to do this walking meditation by having me watch what Catzenbear did."

Later that day, Michael and I were out in the garden, tying up the tomatoes. The roof garden was built on wooden planks and was surrounded by long planter boxes, each filled with different crops: raspberries, strawberries, and blackberries in the berry section; asparagus, tomatoes, carrots, lettuce, and green onions in the vegetable section; and a wide variety of herbs in a third section. The area along the parapet at the edge of the roof was covered with netting to protect Michael's collection of orchids, and there were several boxes along the back of the garden filled with flowers that I cultivated to pick for inside the house.

We had left the door open so Catzenbear and Pooh could join us. I told Michael about how helpful it had been for me to watch the way Catzenbear walked. He laughed when I told him about *paw-paw-paw-paw.*

Just then I turned around and saw Catzenbear jump up to walk along the two-foot-wide parapet. *He really is quite focused when he moves.*

At that moment a butterfly went by, and Catzenbear instinctively leaped for it, landing nimbly back in place but getting way too close to the fifty-foot drop for my comfort.

My heart thumping, I scooped him up and said to Michael that perhaps Catz was not quite ready to be out in the garden.

I sat down next to Poohbear with Catz on my lap. Out of Michael's earshot, Pooh said, "This is a perfect example of what I have been telling you, Kat, about the difference between attention and wisdom. At this stage in his development, Catzenbear focuses only on the butterfly. He must develop wisdom to know how to broaden his awareness to include his surroundings. This will come with experience and training."

"I can see how this applies to Catzenbear, but how does it apply to my meditation practice, Pooh?"

"Excellent question, Kat. You are at the same stage in your practice that Catzenbear is with the butterfly. As you learn to reach deeper levels of concentration, you will experience euphoric states that will be very appealing. Instead of leaping for them, you must understand they are only a small part of a much larger picture. This is why I am here, to help you understand the larger picture."

And then Pooh strolled over to sit on the parapet and enjoy the sunset, while I took Catzenbear back inside.

As our mind becomes
clearer and more lucid
in meditation practice,
hindrances show themselves
more noticeably.

–JOSEPH GOLDSTEIN
Insight Meditation

CHAPTER SIX

Dealing with Dogs

I WAS RELAXING with Poohbear on the couch, leafing through the latest copy of *Spirituality and Health* magazine, when I came across a wonderful picture of a monk sitting in a monastery. In the article below the picture, the monk was quoted saying he had learned to sit perfectly still by watching a cat. Pooh was in his usual spot on the back of the couch, looking over my shoulder, so I held the picture up for him to see it.

"I didn't realize I was following such a venerable tradition, Pooh. Even monks learn how to sit from cats!"

"A great many notable people have been influenced by cats," Pooh responded. "For example, did you know that the famous inventor Nicola Tesla first started wondering about electricity at the age of three, when he saw sparks fly when he petted his cat, Macak? There is also a story about the prophet Muhammad. One day when he was called to prayers, he noticed his cat, Muezza, sleeping on the folds of his sleeve. Rather than disturb the sleeping cat, Muhammad cut off the sleeve of his robe. I could tell you many stories like these."

"And I would love to hear more of them later, Pooh," I said, putting aside the magazine. "Right now, however, it's time for my meditation. Why don't you join me?"

We sat for more than an hour. The story about the monk brought tranquil images into my mind, allowing me to let go of thinking and sit perfectly still. I reached a very deep state of concentration and then experienced my whole body being surrounded by radiant white light. There was a softness to my breathing and a velvet quality in the air around my body. I was filled with gratitude and a deep feeling of peace. When I came out of meditation, I was ecstatic and couldn't wait to tell Pooh.

"I am pleased you had a good experience, Kat. You have been diligent in your efforts, and it is paying off," Pooh said. "However, at this stage in your practice, it is common to experience moments of blissful trance. This is what we call beginner's luck. You must let go of your desire for this altered state, or it will hinder your progress. To attribute this to your skill at this stage in your practice is delusion."

I stood up to put my meditation cushion back on the couch and folded my shawl to drape it over the arm. "I wish you would be happy for me instead of reminding me how much I have to learn, Pooh. And I don't particularly like being told I'm deluded. It was a beautiful moment. Can't you let me bask in it for a while?"

"You are taking this personally, Kat, and this is not what I intended."

"Well, it *feels* personal," I replied.

Pooh jumped to the floor to sit in the sunlight coming in from the window. "I am providing guidance to help you with your practice. Do not identify personally with my words. *You* are not deluded. You may be heading down a path that includes deluded thinking because you lack knowledge of certain practices that will lead to wisdom. That is all I am saying." He paused. "Of course, I am happy that you had a good meditation experience."

This calmed me down a bit, and I felt a little foolish for acting like a spoiled child who wasn't praised for her special achievement. I was pleased with my incredible meditation experience and decided to be satisfied with that.

Just then Catzenbear interrupted us by bouncing into the room, so I picked up a string and began running around the loft with him close on its trail. After we raced back and forth for a few minutes, I was out of breath, so I pulled the end of the string right past Pooh's tail. Catzenbear pounced on Pooh and off they went in a romp. I must admit, it amused me to see my venerable Master act like the playful kitten he once was, before he gained so much wisdom.

Michael and I were having some friends over for dinner that evening, so I decided to leave Pooh and Catz to their playful pursuits and go upstairs to take a nap. While social events were becoming more enjoyable now that my depression was lifting, it still took a lot of energy for me to stay engaged in conversation for several hours. At least I could do that much now, and for this I was very grateful.

When Tom and Linda arrived that evening, we were in the kitchen area giving Catzenbear and Pooh their dinner. Michael opened the door, and to our surprise, their little gray poodle, Nicky, bounded in and raced to the food bowls in the kitchen. I have never seen Pooh move so fast. He was across the loft, up the stairs, and on top of the landing out of Nicky's reach in what seemed like a single bound. Nicky was close on his heels, barking all the way.

In all the commotion I had the presence of mind to grab my camera, so I was able to get a few pictures of Pooh in his full fur-up, back-arched pose. Meanwhile, Linda grabbed Nicky and took him downstairs, putting his leash on to keep him close by. Of course, then Catzenbear immediately came up and leaped on him. They had a great tussle, and then they both settled down for the rest of the evening. Pooh went to sleep on the landing, remaining above us in his safe, superior position until after our guests left.

The next day was Sunday. As I drove to our weekly meditation retreat in Mount Washington, I was looking forward to more blissful sittings like my last one, convinced that I now knew what I was doing. On the way over to Gordon's house, I was laughing about last night's scene with Pooh and Nicky, and thought about how much my mother would have enjoyed watching that little comedy.

The weather was perfect, so I settled down outside for the first sitting. I found myself feeling very emotional. I missed Mom so much, and once I let that feeling in, it became overwhelming.

Finally that passed. Then I felt a surge of anger at Dad for the way he handled Mom as her condition worsened. He treated her like a belligerent child, not his very ill wife of fifty-some years. I became so agitated I wanted to get up and walk out. I could barely sit, and felt I must be crazy to think this meditation stuff was ever going to work. What could Jason, a teacher fifteen years my junior, know about life anyway? Finally I was so exhausted trying to sit through all of this that I fell asleep near the end of the meditation and awoke with the bell.

What a nightmare! I sat quietly through the discussion and left before the next sitting, saying I had promised Michael I would be home early.

I arrived home and threw myself on the couch. Pooh knew I was home too soon, so he suspected something was wrong. He came around the corner and jumped up on the couch with me.

"This is never going to work, Pooh! For every step forward, there are a thousand steps back. I just don't think I can do this anymore. I have had enough!"

"I know this is difficult for you, Kat. Humans have feelings that are not based in the present, and you carry them about as though they are. What is happening to you is that more and more of these feelings are coming up in your meditations, and you do not yet have the skills and understanding to tolerate them."

"That may be, Pooh, but you have feelings, too. I saw how

you reacted to Nicky last night. You seemed pretty anxious about that situation," I responded defensively.

"Exactly my point," Pooh said. "I saw the dog and went into action. I dealt with the situation in the present moment, and after that I did not think about it. I did not second-guess my actions. It was over."

"Well, the incident with Nicky is one thing. You could take action right away. Fight or flight. You decided flight, which was very interesting to me because Nicky is pretty small. Nevertheless, you took action immediately. But a lot of the thoughts coming up for me in my meditation are not things I can act on."

"That is because they are not real. They are just thoughts, and the thoughts are generating more thoughts. And those thoughts are generating feelings. The good news is, now that these thoughts and feelings are coming up, you have more material to work with. You just need new skills to help you learn how to tolerate these feelings in your meditation. This means you have reached a new level in your practice."

I thought about what Pooh had said the next day when I began my meditation. While I was able to observe my feelings better, I had to work at it pretty hard. Even though I tried to concentrate on the still points of my body, I got lost, confused, and tired of trying to sit through a never-ending stream of scenes from the past and projections into the future.

Pooh saw I was struggling, so after my session he said, "The problem you are having, Kat, is that you cannot solve this in the logical way you have solved problems before. As Einstein said, you can't solve a problem at the same level at which it was created. In other words, you cannot solve these problems with your ordinary mind."

"Well, after this last sitting, it's obvious to me I need help. Am I *ever* going to learn how to meditate, Pooh?"

"Take heart, Kat. The feelings coming up in your sittings are no different than the hindrances faced by the Buddha 2600 years ago," Pooh said. "Remember the story about the Buddha sitting under the Bodhi tree for forty-nine days?"

"Yes I do, Pooh, but I'm sure you are going to tell it to me again."

Pooh ignored my attempted humor and went on. "The Buddha fought many formidable battles with Mara, the god of darkness who embodied the hindrances. Ultimately the Buddha defeated Mara and was able to reach a deep state of concentration leading to enlightenment."

"I remember the story. There were five hindrances."

"That is correct, Kat. They are called by different names in various Buddhist texts, but I like to think of them as Clinging, Anger, Sleepiness, Restlessness, and Doubt. I suspect that if you review that terrible sitting you had at Sunday's retreat, you will find that many if not all of these hindrances were present."

I left Pooh, went up to the bedroom to get my notebook, and sat on the bed reviewing my notes about Sunday's sitting. Sure enough, all the hindrances were there. I was clinging to Mom, angry at Dad, restless enough to want to walk out, doubting Jason's ability as a teacher, and at the end, I succumbed to sleepiness. Wow, no wonder my sitting had been such a nightmare!

I came back downstairs, waving my notebook in the air. "You are not going to believe what I found in my notes, Pooh! I encountered every single hindrance in that one sitting."

"I am not surprised, Kat. Often the hindrances will come in groups, although there will also be times when just one hindrance haunts your sitting. Being able to recognize them and learning how to deal with the hindrances is the key to developing the power of your Buddha mind. This is what I meant when I said you cannot figure this out using your ordinary mind. You must learn to open your mind to a much larger vision. This reminds me of the story about the frog who lived all his life in a well . . ."

Just then Catzenbear bounced into the office and jumped up on the desk. He skidded across, knocking off the vase I used to hold pencils. I jumped up and grabbed him before he could escape.

"Look what you did, Catzenbear! You broke the vase Mom gave me! You know you are not supposed to jump up on the desk!" I showed him the broken vase and gave him a little tap on his butt. "This is not acceptable behavior," I said sternly.

I put him on the floor and began picking up the pieces, watching out of the corner of my eye as he tried to slink out of the room. Pooh beat him to the door and reiterated my scolding more physically. After a brief tussle, Catzenbear raced out with Pooh close behind him.

I guess this is one of those instances when I can take immediate action. I was angry at Catzenbear for breaking the vase my mother had given me. I reprimanded him. The vase could be repaired. End of story.

Then I had a flash of insight that showed me what Pooh meant about developing the power of my Buddha mind. I had two choices if I was meditating and this incident came up. One would be to let the memory of the incident pass by without dwelling on it. The other choice would be to begin reminiscing about when Mom gave me the vase, the conversation we had about it, how vital and alive she had been, how much I missed her, how awful her descent into Alzheimer's was, and on and on and on.

I shook my head to clear it. Then I picked up the pieces of the vase and placed them on my bookcase to be glued later. Pooh had talked about opening my mind to a much larger vision. I felt I had just gotten a glimpse of it.

The Hindrances

When we look at wanting,
we experience the part of
ourselves that is never content.

–JACK KORNFIELD
A Path with Heart

CHAPTER SEVEN

Letting Go of Tuna – The Hindrance of Clinging

A FEW DAYS LATER I woke from a dream in which I was the person I used to be, the energetic person who had the stamina and mental acuity that made anything possible. I actually believed I was that person again.

I rubbed my eyes to really wake myself up. Then I looked over at the bookcase beside the bed and saw a copy of the book I'd written just before I got sick. It was never promoted, and most of the other copies of *Winning the Change Game,* my book about how to implement organizational change, were sitting in boxes, stored in the back of the closet. Unfortunately my dream was over, and I was back to reality.

I decided to get up and meditate. In my sitting, I was very attached to thoughts and memories of who I used to be and what my life was like before I got sick. I tried to breathe and move through them, to let them go, but they kept coming back. I continued to sit with the sadness, and eventually the feelings lessened.

After my meditation, I talked to Pooh about the hindrance of clinging.

"I thought clinging was about clinging to things, Pooh, but I saw today that I'm clinging to the person I was in the past. I think if I just do all the right things, I can bring that person back. I'm finding it very hard to accept myself as who I am today."

"Yes, Kat, I see you are sad about what might have been— your career, your active life, and the people you used to know.

You see, cats are not like this. We do not think about the past or the future. We do not yearn."

Pooh thought for a moment. "Do you remember the allergy I had that caused me to lose the fur around my neck?" Pooh asked.

I smiled wryly. "I was so embarrassed by your condition. I guess I just liked thinking of you as my beautiful cat."

Pooh stretched out his legs and repositioned himself on the couch. "I know. But I, on the other hand, continued to take care of my coat and accepted the state it was in. Of course the condition eventually cleared up and my fur grew back, but if it had not, I still would have accepted it."

"I have to remind you, Pooh, that your condition came about as a result of your addiction to tuna." I had been trying out different cat foods, and Pooh had become so obsessed with eating tuna that he wouldn't eat anything else. After he began losing his fur, I took him to the vet to find out what was going on.

"Don't you remember when we went to the vet, and he asked what you were eating? I said the only thing you would eat was tuna. 'Oh well, there you have it,' the vet said. 'He's developed an allergy to tuna because that's all he's eating. This is what's causing him to lose his fur.'"

I stood up and put my hands on my hips to emphasize my point. "So, Poohbear, I don't think your example of how you dealt with the loss of your fur, when you couple it with the fact that it came about because you were addicted to tuna—well, it doesn't seem to be the best example."

"Actually, Kat, it *is* the best example," Pooh replied, "when we compare that situation to what is happening in your meditations. I was craving tuna, you gave me tuna. You were feeding my craving.

"This is exactly what is happening in your mind. Your mind

served up this image of you as you had been. Then you began fueling the flames by thinking more about it, bringing up other examples, thinking about the book you wrote, seeing yourself wearing designer clothes, remembering the places you used to travel, the exciting people with whom you worked. The fire of memory was burning with one log and you kept throwing more fuel on it, fanning the flames. My example is very appropriate."

I thought that sometimes Pooh's cleverness at turning around everything he did into a lesson could be quite annoying, but I remembered the insight I'd had after Catzenbear broke the vase Mom gave me. I had a choice about where I let my mind go. I could choose not to fuel the flames, as Pooh described, so I held my tongue and suggested it was time for tea.

When we got to the kitchen, Pooh jumped up on the counter as I was filling the kettle. He liked to drink from the faucet, so I left it trickling for him.

When he was through drinking, Pooh continued his lesson. "That self you are trying to bring back no longer exists, Kat. It would be like me longing to be a kitten again. That is not possible. You are in pain because you are suffering from delusion and ignorance."

Delusion and ignorance? I was just putting the cat treats in Pooh's bowl. *Now I'm not only deluded, I'm also ignorant?* I paused to consider how many treats I should give him and greatly reduced the number.

We were interrupted when Catzenbear came running up to get some treats, too. There happened to be a toy mouse on the counter, so I threw it to him. He began playing with it and then started chasing his own tail, whirling and whirling until he fell over in a dizzy heap. Pooh and I laughed.

"Great illustration of delusion by Catzenbear," I observed.

"He thinks if he runs as fast as he can he will catch his tail, just like I think I can bring back the way I see myself in the past. Catzenbear may be a little Buddha, but he, too, is deluded."

"You are right, Kat. This is a perfect illustration. I am pleased you see in Catzenbear's tail-chasing how delusion and ignorance contribute to futile behavior. Now, if you have a moment, I would like the rest of my treats."

I smiled and went to the cupboard, getting the treats and adding the requisite number to Pooh's bowl. Then I went upstairs to get dressed and make the bed.

As I was removing the bedcovers, I looked again at my book on the bookcase and thought about how much like chasing my tail my clinging to the past was. *I am causing my own suffering by hanging on to the past.* I knew I had turned a very important corner in my understanding of clinging. Little did I know there was a much more powerful lesson in store for me.

I got up early the next day because Michael was heading out for a fishing trip with the guys and I wanted to see him off. After he left I made breakfast for myself and put out the cat food. Pooh, as usual, came tearing around the corner, but Catzenbear didn't show up. *I must have shut him in the closet by mistake when I was helping Michael get packed.* I went up to the bedroom to open the closet door, expecting him to come bounding out, but he wasn't there.

I went back to get his food dish and walked around the loft shaking it. This was *the* foolproof method for getting his attention, but he still didn't come running. I looked in all the usual places where he might be sleeping and not hear the food bowl.

I expressed my concern to Pooh, and he suggested looking in the garden. *Okay, perhaps Michael left the door open for a few minutes and Catz slipped out.* I walked around the roof garden shaking the food bowl, but no Catzenbear.

Oh God, I hope he hasn't fallen off the roof. I looked over the roof ledge, checking the courtyard on both sides, but saw nothing.

I made one more pass around the garden and searched the entire roof. I made another pass through the loft. Then I went downstairs to search the courtyards. I searched one side of the building, found nothing, and went to the other side, looking under every bush and under all the chairs. Catzenbear was nowhere to be found. I went back upstairs, wishing Michael was home or that I had some way of reaching him. I paced around the loft, wondering what I should do.

Pooh came over and tried to comfort me, but I was so scared I paid no attention to him. I telephoned people in the building asking if anyone had seen Catzenbear. No one had.

Not knowing what else to do, I went downstairs again to search both courtyards, calling Catzenbear's name. There was no response. Then, just as I was about to leave, something made me turn and look under a bush I must have missed, and there he was.

He wasn't moving and didn't seem to be breathing. *Oh please, don't let him be dead.* I reached for him and cried, "Oh my dear little Catzenbear," and he raised his head. I pushed the bush aside and gently picked him up. There was a piece of cactus caught in his fur, and some fur had been scraped off his leg. I put him on my lap and looked him over closely, carefully feeling everywhere to see if anything was broken.

Michael's office was close by on the ground floor, so I took Catzenbear into the office and got a soft towel from the bathroom to wrap him in. No one was there, but I knew Michael kept an extra set of car keys in his desk, so I grabbed them and carried Catzenbear carefully to the car. I placed him tenderly on the car seat and raced to the vet. When we got there I explained that Catzenbear had fallen fifty feet off the roof garden. The vet examined him and said that, while he was pretty roughed up, hitting the cactus most likely broke his fall and saved his life. Except for scrapes and bruises, he was blessedly okay.

I wrapped Catzenbear back in his soft towel and drove home. Pooh was waiting at the door when we came upstairs. I repeated what the vet had told me, assuring Pooh that Catz was going to be okay.

We went into my office, and I gently put Catzenbear down on the couch. Pooh jumped up and started licking him and cleaning his wounds. Catz lay there taking it and, after a little while, began to purr softly. Eventually he fell asleep.

I went to the kitchen to get myself a glass of water and took it to the living room, where I settled into the couch and pulled a blanket over me, more to comfort me than to keep warm. Pooh stopped to drink from his bowl and then followed me to the living room.

"I apologize for ignoring you before, Pooh. I know you were trying to help, but I was too distressed to even pay attention. Weren't you as upset as I was that something might have happened to Catzenbear?" I asked as I sank farther into the couch, completely exhausted.

Pooh jumped up on the couch with me. "Of course, Kat. I love him, too. If he had not returned, I would have retreated to be alone and grieve. While I know loss is a part of life, when it happens there will of course be deep feelings of sadness. Acknowledging one's pain is a necessary part of healing."

Just thinking about the possibility of losing Catzenbear brought tears to my eyes. "This was such a horrible experience, Pooh. I was just beginning to feel alive again, and I have grown so attached to Catzenbear. The love I had for him felt like something

I could count on. Then, wham, Catzenbear was gone."

"I understand, Kat. It would be particularly hard to lose him so soon, just as you had begun to love him so much."

I began to cry in earnest, even though Catzenbear was in the other room. I felt like my heart was breaking. Pooh let me cry for a while before he went on.

"Perhaps you are crying for more than Catzenbear, Kat. Even though your mother is still alive, she is now at a stage with Alzheimer's where she is lost to you. You are grieving that loss, and you are still grieving the loss of your career and your former active life. Adding a totally unexpected loss on top of all of this—even though it has been averted—feels unbearable.

"You are clinging to your love for Catzenbear as a physical being, to this feeling that brings you happiness and comfort. I do not mean to seem callous, Kat, but your belief that this love, this physical being, is necessary for your happiness is a creation of your ordinary mind."

I reached for the tissue box, pulled one out, and wiped my eyes. "I don't understand what you're saying, Pooh. You were the one who suggested we get Catzenbear to help me out of my depression. Now you're saying I don't really need him? This doesn't make any sense to me. What do you mean by that?"

"You fell in love with Catzenbear, and this love helped you begin to feel again, to open up to life. As a result, you are making progress in your meditation practice, which you could not have done in your deeply depressed state. However, it is not enough to replace your depression with your love for Catzenbear. You must replace your personal view of the world with a larger view. You must learn to face life as it is. Let me tell you a story that may help you understand what I am saying."

I curled up and took a long drink of water. After I put the

glass down, Poohbear began his story.

"A mother lost her young son to an illness. She could not accept his death at such an early age, so she went to the Buddha and begged him to bring back her child. The Buddha replied that he would do this if she would bring him a handful of mustard seed. She was certain her son would be saved, for, of course, she could find the mustard seed. Then the Buddha said that the mustard seed must come from a home that had never lost a beloved one. The mother went from house to house for days seeking this mustard seed, finally returning to the Buddha with the understanding that death is a part of everyone's life. When she accepted that reality, she found solace and strength."

I sat quietly and thought about what Pooh had said. *How narrow my view is. Like that mother, I can see only my own pain.* I wanted to believe that somehow life should be different for me, that I should not have to endure my losses, my pain. I was clinging to my specialness, to the view from my ordinary mind.

"Thank you for that story, Pooh. Now I think I would like to meditate for a while to allow me to learn from all that has happened today."

"This is an excellent idea. I would be pleased to sit with you, Kat. Go get your cushion and join me here."

I went to my office to get my cushion. Catzenbear was stretched out on the couch fast asleep, and I stopped to stroke him very lightly, feeling how deeply I loved this little kitten. *My love for him has brought me back to life, but now I need to learn how to comprehend something beyond this physical realm.*

I picked up my cushion and went out to sit with Pooh, to move beyond the illusions of my ordinary mind and unravel the mysteries of the Buddha mind I was seeking.

Life is strictly an adult
education class and this
is the most important
lesson, namely to
cultivate and make the
heart grow.

—AYYA KHEMA
Being Nobody, Going Nowhere

CHAPTER EIGHT

Lovingkindness –
The Hindrance of Anger

I WAS PLANNING to go to the mountains on the weekend for Jason's three-day silent retreat. I had been looking forward to it, as I felt this concentrated period of time was just what I needed to take my practice to a new level.

It had only been two days since Catzenbear's fall, however, so I was thinking about canceling my plan. But Michael assured me he would keep an eye on Catzenbear, so the next day I headed out of Los Angeles and drove up to Idyllwild, a small community nestled in the San Jacinto Mountains. Jason and Jacquelin had recently moved there from L.A. so they could have a place to hold longer retreats.

Their new place was a spacious old wood-shingled lodge surrounded by a forest of pine trees. The large center room had a wood-burning stove and a big river rock chimney, with cozy couches and enough floor space for ten of us to find comfortable spots to meditate. Just off the center room there was a long, open kitchen that allowed everyone to participate in preparing meals. The windows and sliding glass door opened onto an expansive wooden deck overlooking the tree-filled backyard. Later in the day the sun warmed the deck, enticing a number of us to move outside for our afternoon sittings.

After everyone arrived, we all helped make an early dinner and shared what would be our last conversation for three days. Our first sitting began shortly after dinner and lasted an hour.

My sitting was quite peaceful. Even though a number of thoughts and feelings came up, I was able to return to my breath and watch the thoughts pass.

After the sitting, Jason spoke for a short time about the practice of meditation in a retreat setting, and then we went upstairs to silently make our preparations for bed.

The next morning, we were up before dawn, and the first sitting began while it was still dark. This sitting for me was much different from the night before—it was filled with memories of my mother. Jacquelin and her caring manner had reminded me of what Mom was like before she disappeared into Alzheimer's. Mom's was a long, slow decline, and Dad, like so many caregivers, remained in denial for more than a year after it was time for her to go into a care facility. It fell on my shoulders to force the issue. Dad had finally agreed six months ago to place Mom in a nursing home near their home in Dallas.

I became lost in grief for most of my sitting, remembering the awful day we took Mom to the home—how Dad had wrapped Mom's iced tea with a napkin so she could hold on to it without her hands getting cold. I thought about the sad little visits we would make to see her, pretending to be cheerful for each other's sake. I finally came back to the present just before the bell rang.

And so it went, for three days. I experienced the full gamut of emotions throughout the five or six sittings per day, but being in the retreat setting, surrounded by my teachers and fellow meditators, helped me immensely.

I had been a little concerned about being at a silent retreat for three days, but the routine consisted of much more than just sitting. We got up before dawn to sit, then ate breakfast silently. This was followed by a brief rest period and another sitting. Then we would go on a pretty strenuous hike in the mountains of

Idyllwild, again in silence, after which we returned to the lodge and made lunch together, eating it out on the deck. After lunch we had several sittings and a rest period, and then after dinner, Jason shared some of his thoughts on meditation and read us stories he was writing about monks and meditators.

The three days passed so quickly that I was sorry this wasn't a ten-day retreat. I was making real progress in being able to observe my thoughts rather than becoming caught up in them, and this allowed me to reach states of deeper concentration. As I drove down the mountain, I was smiling and feeling very confident about my progress as a meditator.

In fact, I was feeling so good that I found myself wishing that Dad and my sister and brother could get all our families together in a setting like this. When I got home, still in the afterglow of the retreat, I called Dad and invited him to come out for a few days. He said he didn't want to spend the money, and his immediate rejection took me right back to the many times he had rejected me in the past. It wasn't the money, I knew, it was that spending time with me was never a priority for him. And when he did spend time with me, he spent most of it criticizing everything about me.

When the conversation was over, I slammed the receiver down so hard it almost broke. I stomped around the loft, and finally went outside and dug in the garden with a vengeance.

Later I tried to sit, but so much anger, hurt, and bitterness kept coming up about the many times Dad had rejected and criticized me that I finally gave up.

Pooh had been on the couch, observing me as I sat. When I opened my eyes, he said it seemed my sitting had been difficult.

"Difficult, Pooh? It was terrible. I tried to watch my feelings, but there were too many, coming too fast. I am so very angry at

Dad, Pooh."

"Kat, believe it or not, this is a good sign. First you moved from your hopelessness and depression into grieving. Now you are allowing your feelings of anger to come up. Anger is more active than grieving. You are coming back to life."

While what he said might be true, I still needed to do something with all the rage I was feeling. During the past month I had started writing poetry again, so I began getting my anger out on paper. I wrote for days in a burst of creative energy fueled by rage, but this didn't help. The more I wrote, the more ensnared I became. This was *not* how I wanted to feel.

I went over to the couch to sit beside Poohbear and said I was exhausted by these strong emotions. I felt I was regressing rather than making progress in my practice.

"Have compassion for yourself, Kat. You are doing the best you can. Sit with me for a while. Pay attention to your breath and the stillness of your hands. Picture the story about the big ocean the frog saw, and see the vastness that lies beyond your current state of mind."

"What ocean, Pooh? What frog?" I asked.

"Oh yes, I was interrupted and never finished that story did I? It is not important right now, Kat. It is more important to meditate, to learn to let go of your repetitive thoughts."

So we sat. At first I was able to pay attention and relax my body, but then memories flooded up of the way Dad often treated me: his belittling me or his cruel teasing or taunting comments when I was only a little girl. I experienced the events again and again, getting lost in them.

After the sitting I threw my cushion on the couch, narrowly missing Pooh, and said, "I hate this. And now I'm angry about being angry. I'm feeling and acting like a child."

"Who says how you should be acting, Kat? No one is judging. Are you back in this room? Are you present, in this moment?"

I looked at him and took a deep breath. Then another deep breath. I realized I was just coming back to the present, into the room, onto the couch; aware that I was sitting next to him.

"Good. Now you are here. This is a very good time for you to learn how to examine your meditations more closely. I want you to understand why this flooding of memories is happening to you. So now, please go back and revisit your meditation experience. Pay attention to where you were, when it was, who you were at that time. Take as much time as you need to do this," Pooh instructed.

I closed my eyes and did as he said. In reviewing what I could remember from the sitting, I saw two different scenes.

I began telling him what I saw. "I am in the kitchen of our house in Kodiak, Alaska. I am five years old. My parents are playing cards. I know how to play with my Old Maid cards, but I desperately want to join them at the kitchen table and be part of their adult game. I beg repeatedly, and then Dad says, "Okay, how would you like to play 52-Pickup?" I am ecstatic. "Yes," I cry excitedly. I begin climbing up in the chair as he picks up the deck. He makes a big show of shuffling the cards, and I can hardly wait for him to deal the hands. Then he laughs and throws them all over the floor. "'Okay," he says, "pick 'em up.""

Pooh asked, "How did you react?"

I opened my eyes. "I didn't react. I learned at an early age, earlier than five years old, that I had to pretend Dad's kidding didn't bother me. If I showed I was hurt or angry, Dad would storm out of the room, saying he just couldn't deal with me when I acted like that. Then Mom would tell me to apologize to Dad for hurting his feelings. I had to develop the ability to split off my feelings in order to survive."

"You said there was another scene, Kat. Describe that one for me."

As soon as Pooh said that, I closed my eyes and immediately landed in a completely different time and place. "This time I'm on the patio of my house in California with Dad and my future husband. I am thirty-seven years old, and the three of us are having a conversation about something, when Dad turns to my future husband and says, "You know, Kathy would be pretty good looking if she just got her teeth straightened and had more of a chin.""

Pooh said, "Open your eyes, Kat. Come back to the room."

I took a few deep breaths and looked around. It took a few more seconds to become fully aware that I was sitting on the couch next to Pooh.

"So, do you see what is happening?" Pooh asked. "You are allowing yourself to be pulled into another world, a world that doesn't exist anymore, with people and a self who do not exist today. You were unable to react then, and you are unable to react in your vivid memory of these events. You are caught in what the Buddha called the Wheel of Samsara, reliving the same events over and over again."

Pooh turned his body to face me more directly, to emphasize the importance of what he was saying. He wanted to be certain I was paying attention.

"The way to get out of the wheel is to become curious about this anger and this hurt and this humiliation. These feelings you are having are *not* you. Do not participate in the scene. Do not be overcome by what is happening in it. Step back and look at it from a distance."

He repeated his instruction once again. "Be curious about the feeling you are having. Learn to investigate it. As an example, think about the way I am curious about anything new that comes into the loft."

Finally I smiled a little. I'd seen Pooh being curious about anything new that came into the loft. I'd also seen Pooh threatened by something as innocuous as a new piece of sculpture Michael brought up from his studio. Pooh would crouch down, ready to run in an instant.

"Well Pooh, I'm not sure this is the best example. At times you don't seem very curious. I would say that sometimes you even appear threatened."

"Yes, well possibly, if it is something I do not recognize. Sometimes I decide to be protective and ready to defend myself in case it should become dangerous," Pooh replied.

"You mean like Nicky, the little gray poodle that was smaller than you?" I teased.

"He was not that much smaller. I was just being a good host and getting out of his way. But no matter. The point is, after I see that whatever it is cannot harm me, I become curious. I examine it very closely from all angles, trying to understand it fully. Are you getting the connection?"

"Pretty obvious, even for me," I laughed. Then I realized I was present, and my anger had passed.

At my meditation group the next day, some of the same old memories came up in my first sitting. I tried being curious and exploring the emotions, with some success. But then the memory of Dad saying I could almost be pretty if only my teeth were straighter and I had more of a chin came back, and I got caught up in the story again.

I told Jason what was happening and what I was trying to do. I said I was trying to be curious about the memories, but when the feelings became too strong, I would lose my ability to be curious and become overwhelmed by the story and the feelings it brought up. He asked about the theme of the meditation. At first I said it was anger, but I realized the anger was being fueled by my feeling hurt and humiliated. *I'm getting better at this*, I told myself.

"Good," he said. "You are learning to look at anger more closely to see what is fueling it. This is a perfect opportunity to practice exploring the roots of this hindrance further. As these feelings come up, you might ask yourself questions about them. What is the texture, the tone of them? Questions like these will help you remain curious and allow you to investigate the story and your feelings further. This investigating will help you get more information and see things you may have not seen before."

In my next sitting, the same memories surfaced once again. This time I allowed the story to keep running, and as my anger at Dad came up, I asked myself about the texture and tone of the feeling. I felt how rough and harsh it was, and I felt how my body responded to it: sometimes my stomach would tighten, other times I would stop breathing. I took a deep breath and let it out slowly, and then another deep breath in and out. The story was still present but the scene had shifted, as though I were looking at it from another angle. It was just a story about a woman who made a decision as a young girl that it was not acceptable to speak her truth. Each person was acting on decisions they made long ago about how they needed to be in the world. I saw how my version of the story could morph and change in an instant; that if I could tolerate uncomfortable feelings and explore them further, I might see different sides of it, like circling around the scene for another view.

I relaxed and thought about … nothing. I moved into a very deep state and experienced a feeling of deep bliss all over my body. *So this is what it feels like when I allow the stories to keep running until I am able to see more sides of them. What seems like a hindrance is really more like a hall of mirrors—if I look at only one of the mirrors, I am holding on to only one interpretation of the story and the hindrances related to that interpretation.*

On the drive home I thought about Dad and how much he and Mom loved each other, how they were each other's whole life for over fifty years. I remembered them dancing at their fiftieth anniversary party. They were so lovely together. When they stopped dancing, he rested his chin on her head, and they smiled and held each other. He knew this was the last party, the last time Mom would be able to function in public.

I began to feel compassion, and tears rolled down my face. "Oh Dad, I know you did the best you could. That is what I really wanted to say when I was pushing you to come out here. I know you love me even if it is hard for you to show it. And I know you are heartbroken about Mom."

And then I felt compassion for the little girl I had been and for all the children who are hurt by so many thoughtless or violent acts—including my own parents. Dad's father had been shot to death on the street in the small Texas town where he grew up. Dad was ten years old. And Mom's father had left home on a business trip when she was two years old and never came back. So many forms of shame, humiliation, and violence just in our little family.

I thought about the lessons I'd read on "lovingkindness," a practice that emphasizes feelings of love, happiness, and compassion. I also thought about how uninterested I'd been when I'd read those lessons. I realized now that I had not been ready to forgive. I had wanted to hold on to my righteous anger. And now, what was I so angry about? Was it what had happened to me? Was it what had happened to Dad? Was it what had happened to

Mom? Or was it what had happened in the stories I was holding on to about my life? Were there other understandings, other mirrors that might also be valid?

When I got home, I went to the bookshelf and took out Sharon Salzburg's book, *Lovingkindness*. I opened it to a page at random, and read:

> The Buddha taught that the forces in the mind that bring suffering are able to temporarily hold down the positive forces such as love or wisdom, but they can never destroy them. The negative forces can never uproot the positive, whereas the positive forces can actually uproot the negative forces. Love can uproot fear or anger or guilt, because it is a greater power.

I put the book down and cried softly for a long time. When I was finished, I was not the same person I had been for the past few weeks. *The goodness, the positive forces are always there. Wow. This is our Buddha nature.*

I looked for Pooh to tell him about my big breakthrough and let him know how much I appreciated his wisdom and compassion. I found him asleep on the couch with Catzenbear tucked in beside him, a perfect example of lovingkindness if ever there was one.

Sometimes just bringing
an interested awareness to
sleepiness itself will dispel it and
bring clarity and understanding.

—JACK KORNFIELD
A Path with Heart

CHAPTER NINE

Watching the Water –
The Hindrance of Sleepiness

NOW THAT MY ANGER no longer had me by the throat, I was making progress again with my sittings. Many times I was actually able to let go of thinking and experience some blissfully quiet and calm moments.

I was enjoying just such a sitting when I realized I must have dozed off, because I woke with a start when Catzenbear leaped up on me. I hadn't been sleepy at the beginning of the sitting.

Since dozing off had occurred in several of my recent meditations, I decided to ask Pooh about it. I went to the kitchen to make some tea and poured some cat treats into his bowl. This was always the easiest way to find him.

I sat at the long breakfast bar off the kitchen to drink my tea. Michael had used his favorite tile for our extensive bar and counter-space, bringing the whole kitchen alive with its glossy deep blue color, and I had found the perfect rug for the wood floors, a handmade light blue rug with a variety of beautifully colored trout on it. I loved seeing Catzenbear and Pooh curled up on that rug when we ate at the counter, as we often did.

After Poohbear had finished eating, he jumped up on one of the barstools and leaped on the counter. I told him about how I was falling asleep in my meditations and asked him why this might be happening.

"Well, there are three causes for sleepiness in meditation," Pooh said, as he began to clean his whiskers. He paused to list them for me. "One is that there is something you do not want to deal with. It is only natural for you to become sleepy when things are too difficult for you to think about. Sleeping is what you have been doing during your long illness."

I interrupted him. "I know that sleeping a lot was necessary for me when I was sick, Pooh, but I have more energy now. I don't think I'm using sleep as an escape. You said there were three reasons. What are the other two?"

"The second reason is that it is difficult to maintain a calm state if you do not know how to remain alert. And the third reason is that you may genuinely be tired and need to sleep." Having answered my question to his satisfaction, Pooh left me to think about it and headed out to the roof garden for a nap.

Several days later I had another sitting in which I felt very calm and went into a deep state. Thinking stopped and I experienced a wonderful feeling of blissfulness. My breathing was calm, my heart centered, my body relaxed, and my mind totally unoccupied. Then once again I woke with a start when I slipped off my cushion.

At the retreat on Sunday, I decided to ask Jason for his views on this problem of sleepiness that I was encountering. He said that tranquil states can be challenging for new meditators because we will often fall asleep in them. *Hmmm, that was just what Poohbear said about how difficult it was to remain alert in a calm state. It was comforting to know that both my teachers were on the same wavelength.* Jason told us there is a lot to be gained from these states if we can learn to remain slightly more awake while we are in them.

The group discussed ways to stay alert, such as our old standbys of being aware of our body or paying attention to our breathing. Someone said they read about monks who would sit on the edge of a well to keep them sufficiently awake while meditating. This seemed a bit extreme—after all, we were not trying to avoid sleepiness completely. We just wanted to learn to work with it.

On the drive home I thought about the sittings in which I had fallen asleep. I had lost my ability to pay attention, so again the issue was how to remain in a calm, tranquil state and still remain alert. *But a calm, tranquil state was the prelude to sleep, wasn't it? Hmmm, this was obviously going to require more thought.*

It was almost time for bed when I got home, so I decided to take a bath before going to sleep. As I was running the bathwater, Pooh jumped up on the sink counter for a drink, so I turned the water on for him.

Then Catzenbear jumped up on the edge of the tub, which he could now do without slipping in, unlike the first time he tried when he had an unexpected swim. What was it about Maine Coon cats and their attraction to running water?

I sank into my nice warm bath and watched Catzenbear lean forward to drink the bath water as it came up within his reach. The first time he did this I pictured him toppling in, flailing and scratching, as I remembered how frantic he'd been when he fell in by himself. But now he was an adept ledge-sitter, so we coexisted in peaceful bliss at the watering hole.

When I got out of the tub and opened the drain, Catz, as usual, waited until most of the water was gone and then jumped in so he could watch the last of it swirl down the drain. I watched as he stared, completely absorbed and fascinated with the small whirlpool.

Now that is paying attention with a capital "P" and a capital "A." That's the kind of concentration I need to keep me from falling asleep in my sittings. I mentioned this to Pooh, and he replied,

"Well, I could have told you that visualizing something and paying close attention to it will help you stay alert, but it is always better when you discover it for yourself."

"In this case I agree with you, Pooh. Watching Catzenbear staring at that whirlpool has provided a powerful image to use in my meditation, and I have to admit it was nice to make my own discovery."

The next day I had a sitting in which I reached that calm, tranquil state that was usually my prelude to falling asleep, so I visualized Catzenbear watching the water go round and round, down the drain, and I became absorbed in the visual of the swirling water. I was able to stay attentive and maintain my energy. Ultimately I reached a very deep state of concentration.

After the sitting I told Pooh I was able to become absorbed by concentrating on the image of the water, just as Catzenbear had demonstrated in the bathtub. Of course, Pooh reminded me that Catzenbear was not the teacher, he was merely the example.

"You know, Pooh, my other teachers don't feel it is always necessary to remind me that they are the teacher," I said.

"That may be true, Kat, but they do not know you as well as I do. I see how easy it is for you to dismiss the importance of a teacher once you think you have learned the lesson. This practice is so rich and layered that I do not want you to think you understand it prematurely. This is not something you can master by learning a few steps and then go on about your life. I am helping you open your mind far beyond what you can imagine. And since you cannot imagine it, how can you decide for yourself when you have reached the end?"

I knew enough by now to realize that Pooh was speaking the truth. In order to escape criticism from my dad, I had learned at an early age to be independent. And I had learned not to trust people who might want to control me, like teachers and possible mentors. My belief that I had to be "better than, smarter than" everyone else had made me a workaholic and had eventually led me to illness and depression. Clearly, there had to be a better way.

"You're right, Pooh, it's certainly not easy for me to admit I need help, nor is it easy for me to accept the guidance of a teacher. But I know it is time for me to change this behavior, and I know enough now to suspect that there really is no end to this path I am on. So I suppose I might as well just relax and enjoy the journey—and let you be the teacher."

Later in the week, I drove to a temporary placement agency in Pasadena to take the battery of tests they required before they would send me out on temp jobs. I really needed to work to help with expenses, but since I didn't know how well I could perform back out in the world, I had decided to try temporary work. But first I had to jump through the agency's testing hoops, and I had been dreading this all week.

Once I arrived at the agency, I worked hard to stay centered and not let the pressure of performing against a timer derail my ability to focus. I had to take word processing and basic math tests, and if this wasn't degrading enough, the tests weren't all that easy for me. I wasn't back to normal yet when it came to being able to concentrate for long periods of time, and I still had trouble dealing with numbers. My biggest accomplishment to date was that I'd begun balancing my checkbook again.

The testing took over three hours, and by the time I finished, I had a terrible headache. The agency was located in a mall with new carpeting that was out-gassing formaldehyde, so every time someone opened the door, fumes came into the testing area. This out-gassing of chemicals from new carpeting and other renovations in my office was what had triggered my chronic fatigue, and I was still susceptible to it. I was able to keep going only because I was determined to pass those tests. While I knew I'd probably be physically ill from toxic exposure during the next few days, I put that thought out of my mind and concentrated on the task at hand.

When I was finished, I walked outside for some fresh air before going down to the underground parking lot to find my car. I breathed deeply and brought myself to the present moment, instead of continuing to ruminate about how I had done on the tests.

I was exhausted by the time I got home, but it seemed important to sit so I could reorient myself to the present moment. After a while I woke up with a start and realized I had once again fallen asleep during my sitting. *Let's see, three causes of sleepiness: avoidance of feelings, unable to maintain an alert state in a calm sitting, and, oh yes, just plain tired.*

"This time I fell asleep because I'm just plain tired," I said to Pooh as I picked up my cushion and put it on the couch.

"Well, you are dealing with a lot, Kat. I am sure today was stressful for you, and that you are truly exhausted. There is no need to look for any hidden meanings. As the saying goes, sometimes a banana is just a banana."

"Where on earth did you get that, Pooh?"

"I heard it on television. I pay attention to everything around here," he said, as he headed off to the kitchen.

When the mind is
restless, it is the proper
time for cultivating
tranquility, because an
agitated mind can easily
be quieted by it.

—NYANAPONIKA THERA,
translator
*The Five Mental Hindrances
and Their Conquest*

CHAPTER TEN
Catzenbear's Tranquility – The Hindrance of Restlessness

IT WAS OFFICIAL: I had passed the tests. The temp agency gave me a regular assignment two days a week processing payroll for Avon, so I was back in the workforce. I smiled when they called me about the assignment, remembering the tiny little lipstick samples Mom let my sister and me play with when she was an Avon Lady. She would have gotten a kick out of the fact that I was going to be working at the assembly plant where I could watch all the Avon products coming down the assembly line.

I was to begin my new assignment on Tuesday. For the next few days I was diligent about sticking to my meditation schedule, figuring I would need my sitting routine now more than ever since I would be back out in the "real" world.

A new pattern began to emerge in my sittings. Something I couldn't quite identify was making me feel anxious. This was not a physical restlessness I was dealing with. My body wasn't feeling twitchy. This was a restlessness in my mind. The feeling of anxiety was so strong I found myself ending my sittings rather abruptly, without even realizing I had made the decision to do so.

I decided it might be helpful to talk to Pooh about this, and found him relaxing in the garden, watching the birds peck at the blackberries on the vines. I shooed the birds away from our lovely crop of berries, and sat down next to him.

"As you have no doubt observed, Pooh, I've been cutting my sittings short lately. I'm feeling restless. When I looked up restlessness in one of my books, it said it's usually in response to worry."

The birds having flown off, Poohbear settled down with a small sigh and turned his attention to my plight. "It is true that worry may be one of the sources of restlessness, Kat. Perhaps it might help to talk about it. Tell me, what are your worst fears right now?"

I thought for a moment and began to count my concerns on my fingers.

"Well, first, while I am grateful to have actually gotten this job, I think I'm afraid I'll be stuck doing this kind of work forever. Second, I'm still worried about money. What I'm being paid won't really help that much. Third is my health. I'm exhausted at times, and I'm scared the whole chronic fatigue thing will start up again."

"So—work, money, health. These are big concerns, Kat."

"This is true, Pooh, but these worries are nothing new to me. I've been able to watch these same worries in other sittings and was able to let them go. Why would they suddenly create such anxiety now?"

"Well then, perhaps it is something more, something you have not allowed yourself to see before." Pooh sat up to take a swat at the fly that had been annoying him. I thought for a moment that he would turn the fly swatting action into some sort of lesson, but he just went on to say, "If this is the case, then there is a fight going on inside you as to whether you want to see what it is or keep it buried. This is the restlessness. If you decide you want to investigate it, you will need to learn more skillful means to handle that. Perhaps you should bring this matter up at your meditation retreat tomorrow."

Acting on Pooh's suggestion, on Sunday at the retreat I brought up the experience I was having with this feeling of restlessness, this undefined anxiety. Jason suggested that when I felt overwhelmed by such strong feelings, I could develop more tolerance for them by occasionally going back to the still points of my body. *Once again, using the still points to ground myself would help me weather the emotional storm.* I smiled. This was something I already knew how to do—something so simple I had overlooked it. I was going to try this in our next group sitting, but perhaps because I was at the retreat and felt such support, my sitting was very calm and uneventful.

Tuesday morning I started at Avon. Peggy, the manager of the agency, met me at the Avon facility in Pasadena to show me around. She introduced me to everyone as the temp who would be processing payroll. I put my mind on autopilot, learned the routine, and got through the day without letting my feelings well up. It would have been so easy to start comparing the quiet, low-key, ordinary person I was now with the fast-paced, insightful, forceful person I used to be.

The day was long and demanding, both physically and emotionally. Fortunately, my Tuesday night meditation group was not meeting that week. I was exhausted when I got home, too tired to eat or talk, and went right to bed.

The next afternoon I took my cushion into my writing room and settled down to meditate. In the beginning my thoughts were scattered. I watched different scenarios take place and managed to let them go. I started feeling relaxed. Then, without warning, I felt extremely anxious, and I really wanted to end the sitting. Instead I went back to the still points in my body and that calmed me down a bit.

I continued to sit and tried to get distance from the feeling of anxiety. I tried being curious about it and began exploring where it might be in my body. My body felt tight all over, but the tightness was mostly in my chest. I realized I was holding my breath, so I began taking some long, slow, deep breaths. This made me feel better.

And then again the overwhelming anxiety came up, and again I wanted to end my sitting. My thoughts shifted to the Buddha. I saw him sitting under the Bodhi tree and remembered the stories about the Buddha's battles with Mara, the god who personifies the hindrances to meditation. Fears had assaulted the Buddha in the guise of demons, dreadful screaming sounds, floods, hurricanes, avalanches, lighting bolts, and, worst of all, a silent, all-enveloping darkness. And he sat through it all. *Surely what is lurking in my meditation couldn't be any worse than that.*

And yet, to me it was. I could barely stay on my cushion. Then I remembered the rest of the Buddha's story. When Mara saw the Buddha was winning, he screamed at him, "Get up from this seat, Siddhartha! It does not belong to you, but to me!"

The Buddha answered Mara's claim by touching the earth with his fingertips, whereupon the ground quaked and a great roar burst forth. "I, Earth, bear you witness. Buddha, this seat is yours!" Mara and all his forces fled, and the Buddha continued to sit until he reached enlightenment.

I touched the wood floor with my fingertips and resolved to remain on my cushion. An image popped into my mind of Catz sleeping on the kitchen counter in the large blue bowl that Pooh and I laughingly referred to as Catzenbear's tranquility bowl. That image brought with it the quality of tranquility, and I began to feel calm. I could still sense the anxiety lurking around the edges, but I was able to remain in a very calm state, visualizing

Catzenbear curled up asleep in his blue bowl.

Poohbear was on the couch next to me when I opened my eyes, and I shared my experience with him. I told him I was able to deal with the anxiety in the meditation but still felt it lurking around me. It seemed more ominous than any of my usual thoughts and worries.

Pooh looked thoughtful as he pushed one of the pillows out of his way in order to look at me more directly. "This anxiety that is frightening you so, what is its name?"

"I don't know," I answered.

"Yes you do. You can name it if you allow yourself to, Kat."

And then he commanded, "Name it now."

I hesitated and then said, "I'm not good enough." Lowering my head for a second, I looked up at Pooh and repeated, "I'm not good enough." Then quietly, as if now used to the idea, I softly said, "I am not good enough."

We sat in silence for a long time until I spoke.

"Pooh, all my life I've been able to avoid naming my anxiety, my fear. First by receiving accolades by being a workaholic, and then, when I was sick, I avoided naming it by putting all my energy into getting well. Depression was just another way of repressing my big secret. And now here I am back out in the work world without my workaholic ability to split off my feelings and obsessively tackle any problem. Won't I feel naked out there without my Wonder Woman bracelets?" I was only half joking about the Wonder Woman reference. She had been one of my favorite comic book characters, precisely because her bracelets made her so invulnerable.

Pooh waited a moment to make sure he had my attention. "No, Kat. By naming your fear, you take its power away. So many people leave the practice at this point because they cannot deal with these strong feelings. It is unfortunate because when they can name their fear, it loses its power. I am very proud of you for staying the course."

My mind was still whirling from my discovery. The underlying core belief driving me like a mad woman into one achievement after another, into an illness, and then into depression was all to hide the fact that deep down I believed I was not good enough.

"It's hard to believe something so empty and so untrue could have been my driving force all my life," I said.

"And now you know," Pooh replied.

"Yes, and now I know." I smiled and laughed out loud. The tension and anxiety were gone. Could it really be that simple? I suspected it was not, but I was certainly willing to bask in the moment. I knew more layers would be revealed in the future, but for now I breathed a deep, fresh breath and said, "Yes, and now I am free to feel good enough."

Michael would be home soon, so I picked up my cushion and put it on the couch. The Buddha was able to touch the earth. I lived in a loft three stories above the earth, but I, too, had been able to touch my fingers on the wood floor and reach deep into a connection to Buddha mind that I had not known was possible. Once there I was able to release another of Mara's obstacles, not the demons or floods or screams or darkness inflicted upon the Buddha, but something more debilitating to me: an unfounded core belief that I was not good enough.

I stood up and went to the kitchen to make some tea, and there was Catzenbear on the counter, sound asleep in his tranquility bowl. *In his young state of Buddha nature, Catzenbear is a perfect example of how tranquility triumphs over restlessness.* I smiled at the thought and leaned over to give him just the lightest kiss on his little nose.

And when he sees himself free
of these five hindrances, joy
arises; in him who is joyful,
rapture arises.

—NYANAPONIKA THERA,
translator
*The Five Mental Hindrances
and Their Conquest*

CHAPTER ELEVEN

Poohbear's Rapture – The Hindrance of Doubt

AFTER A FEW WEEKS of doing the payroll at Avon, I realized I could, in fact, work two days a week without becoming physically ill. This was a big achievement.

I began taking on more responsibility than I really needed to as a temp, just because it felt good to be solving problems no one else caught. I even skipped my Tuesday meditation group to stay late and design a process to improve Avon's payroll system.

On Sunday Michael and I had a commitment to attend a family party. While I wanted to go to my Sunday afternoon retreat, I knew it was important to Michael for me to go with him, so I skipped Sunday's retreat as well.

The next Tuesday I forgot to take my casual clothes to work and would have had to rush home to change before going to my meditation group. I was tired and decided to skip this one, too, and get to bed early.

By the weekend I was in an agitated state. Instead of going to the group on Sunday, I decided to embark on a thorough house-cleaning. Catzenbear ran to my office to escape the vacuum cleaner, as I moved couches, tables, and chairs to make sure the vacuum missed not one speck of dust. Confused by my frantic cleaning, Catz jumped up on the couch to hide behind Pooh. Pooh reassured him he had seen me like this before. He explained that in the past, when I became frustrated about something, this was the way I dealt with it.

Finally I wore myself out.

I joined Pooh and Catzenbear on the couch, exhausted, and tried to take a nap but I wasn't sleepy. I decided to read for a while. The side table was piled with books, as usual, so I picked up the closest one—Ayya Khema's *Being Nobody, Going Nowhere*, a practical guide to meditative insight. Glancing through the table of contents, there in the section on hindrances the words *Skeptical Doubt* jumped out at me. Okay, I thought, and turned to the chapter on skeptical doubt.

It seemed there were two kinds of doubt. The first was about the meditation practice. Was the Buddha really enlightened? Were the teachings really true? And were one's teachers perpetuating the teachings correctly?

Well, well, well. I smiled. It hit me that at the same time I got back out into real life, I began doubting that I needed my practice of meditation. The longer I stayed away from my meditation group, the easier it was to let it go and find seemingly justifiable excuses not to attend. I was falling right back into my old familiar ways of dealing with real life.

I read on and got another solid hit.

More damaging for one's personal growth was the second type of doubt: self-doubt, when you doubted your own abilities and your spiritual aptitude. *Yes!* I was back in the real world with my former out-in-the-world mindset back in charge, and I had discovered that the two ways of being couldn't coexist. One had to go, and I gave up my meditation practice without even realizing I was doing it.

I really wanted to talk about this, so I nudged Pooh with my foot to wake him up. It took a few tries, but he finally opened his eyes. "What is it now, Kat?" he asked sleepily. "Have you decided to shampoo all the couch cushions?"

I smiled at him. "I guess I have been a bit frenzied this morning, haven't I? I've just been reading something that helped me see what's going on. I believed I was handling myself well at my new job, but without realizing it I slipped back into what was familiar, my old workaholic behavior. From there it was easy to forget all about my health and personal goals. My meditations became mechanical, and when any reason came up to skip my meditation group meetings, no problem, I just didn't go. I'm astonished at how easily I turned my back on something as significant as my meditation practice, something that has been such a big part of my recovery from depression."

Pooh sat up, disturbing Catzenbear's sleep. Catz looked around and moved farther into the corner, where he curled up and settled down again. Pooh walked over to my end of the couch and sat down.

"Do not feel too badly, Kat. This problem of doubt happens to many new practitioners. Feel good that you woke up. Diversions are your test to see if you can surrender your whole being to becoming the master of your mind."

"And if I can?" I asked.

"Your old behaviors and ways of seeing the world will become just that—old. You will be able to be in the active world *and* maintain your mental, emotional, spiritual, and physical health."

"I see why this is so hard for me right now, Pooh. I have always been someone who does more than anyone else, so it is very hard for me to accept that sitting is more important than doing. But—and this may seem like a silly play on words—the reality is that I am doing something far more important than anything else I could do while I am sitting, something that impacts everything in my life."

"So you are learning the importance of choosing to *be* rather than *do*, Kat. This is the proper order, because if you cannot *be*, you cannot *do*," Pooh responded with a grin, enjoying our little wordplay.

"Exactly," I replied with a laugh.

And so when Tuesday came, I was the first one to arrive at our regular meditation retreat. Jacquelin greeted me with a warm hug and told me how glad she was to see me, and, just like that, I was back on track.

After our first sitting, I brought up my struggles with doubt. I said that, in my case, I hadn't even seen it as doubt. It was more like my practice faded from my mind once I went back to my old patterns in the outside world. Jason said that doubt can be useful if we express it. It is a natural part of our development as meditators to reconsider and question our conviction. I realized that in a way I had not doubted enough. I'd pushed my doubts away and ignored them. I said that instead of coming to the group to discuss my doubts, I had taken up fanatic vacuuming instead. We all had a good laugh, and Jacquelin, smiling, said the sangha—our spiritual community—would benefit greatly by having cleaner floors, and suggested I keep both as practices.

Pooh was waiting for me in my writing room when I came home, so I made a cup of tea and joined him on the couch to review the evening.

"Well Pooh, it seems that doubt in and of itself is not bad. It is when I push it away and don't acknowledge it that I get into trouble."

"By trouble, do you mean that you go back to your busy ways and tear the loft apart to keep from admitting that you are having some doubts?" Pooh asked with a sly smile.

"Sometimes I wonder why I even bother to drive all the way to Mount Washington for my retreats, Pooh. All the answers are right here. I guess I just need confirmation from one who walks on two legs instead of four," I said grinning back at him.

"Indeed. I am not insulted by your need for reassurance from your own kind. If you will remember, I was the one who told you to find a human teacher. Validation is important at this stage of your growth."

"Ah yes, there's the behavior I know so well, reminding me once again who is the teacher and who is the student," I said, laughing. I got up and, putting my hands in prayer position, bowed deeply to him. "It's late, dear Master, and I have to work tomorrow. This has been quite a long day."

"Yes it has," Pooh said, nodding back to me. "However, I could do with a drink from the faucet and a little snack before we turn in."

The next day I was asked to go the temp agency office instead of Avon, to help with a special accounting project. This meant I was back in the environment with new carpet out-gassing. Great. I immediately got a terrific headache and had trouble concentrating and working at a pace fast enough to suit Peggy, the agency manager. She criticized me for being so slow, and I watched myself go from anger, to craving for who I used to be, to doubting myself—all in the space of a nanosecond.

After I passed through my little time tunnel, I asked Peggy if she would show me a better way to do this task, since I hadn't done it before. She jumped in and completed several batches for me. Letting her show me how to do it her way made her comfortable, and gave me time to quietly take a couple of deep breaths and relieve my headache. Amazingly, I was actually, as Pooh had promised, gaining wisdom. I didn't have to work nearly as hard if I stopped trying to prove I was smarter than everyone else. What a revelation!

At the end of the day, Peggy said she was having everyone over on Friday for a farewell party for Marie, one of our coworkers, and asked if I'd like to join them. I surprised myself by saying yes, and as I walked to the parking garage, I actually felt happy for the first time since I started the job.

Michael was in the kitchen when I got home, so I told him about my day. He knew I'd been struggling with doing this type of rote work, so when I told him I was going to a little party at Peggy's on Friday, he was surprised. I smiled and said I had figured out this wasn't really such a big deal. They were nice people, I was getting back out into the world, and I was actually learning how to make my life easier.

Pooh overheard my conversation with Michael and was waiting for me when I walked into my office, smiling like he knew something I didn't know.

"You are now realizing the power of this practice, Kat. You have broken through into accepting the world as it is, not as you would like it to be. We talked at the very beginning of our journey about the delusion of ordinary mind. Allow me to tell you a little story that illustrates what happens when you break through that delusion."

He began, "There was a frog who had lived all his life in a well . . ."

Just then Michael called out that dinner was ready, and Pooh beat me to the kitchen, once again leaving the frog story for another time.

I couldn't find Poohbear after dinner to get the rest of the story, so I decided to meditate before going to bed. My sitting was unremarkable in that I didn't have to battle much with the hindrances. I just sat and watched them go by. No restlessness, no sleepiness. My mind felt calm and quiet. And then a tingling of bliss and rapture came over me, followed by warm, golden light.

Just another ordinary sitting. I smiled to myself as I got up to go to bed.

Michael was in the living room watching a movie on television, so I kissed him goodnight and went up to the bedroom. There was Pooh, spread out on his back among the covers on our bed, on top of one of my Zen poetry books.

Now that is rapture. This is what it looks like when you are able to let go of the hindrances.

I picked up the books and papers and moved Poohbear to the bottom of the bed. He stirred a little and then went back down into his deep, luxurious sleep.

I climbed into bed and settled down to join him.

Buddha Mind

Use your life
to wake you up.

—PEMA CHODRON
The Wisdom of No Escape

CHAPTER TWELVE

Gaining Wisdom

I SET ASIDE most of the day on Saturday to get ready for our week-long vacation in the mountains. We were leaving on Sunday and I had a lot of packing to do. But first, since I'd gone to sleep wondering about the frog story Poohbear kept bringing up, I went looking for him. I wanted to hear the rest of the story.

I found Pooh meditating on the blue couch in my office, so I decided to join him. As I settled down on my cushion, I remembered the day less than a year ago when I had picked up *The Tibetan Book of Living and Dying.* That was the first time I talked to Pooh about the difference between ordinary mind and Buddha mind.

As I closed my eyes, my heart filled with gratitude for how far we had come together. A feeling of contentment came over me, and I entered a profoundly quiet place of no time, no thought, no movement. Suddenly a brilliant white space filled my vision, and I was surrounded by tiny golden lights. A myriad of colors began to flow through the tiny lights, as my body tingled all over. I literally felt, quite pleasantly, as if my head were exploding into a million pieces. The visions and feelings passed as suddenly as they had appeared, and again there was stillness. I watched as thoughts began to come and go, passing by like leaves floating down a stream. As I became more aware of my physical body, I felt my breath moving in and out.

When I opened my eyes, Poohbear was watching me. "I see it is time for me to finish the story about the frog in the well," he said.

"That's why I came to find you, Pooh."

"Well then, let me begin and finish it this time. It is a very short story, but the timing has not been right to tell it before, or we would not have been interrupted. It comes from your *Tibetan Book of Living and Dying*, the book you were reading the day we began this journey."

So Pooh was thinking about that day, too.

"It's hard to believe how much things have changed since we began, isn't it, Pooh?"

"Yes, Kat, perhaps we will talk about this after I finish the story. The story begins when an old frog who had lived all his life in a dank well was visited one day by a frog from the sea.

"'Where do you come from?' asked the old frog in the well.

"'From the great ocean,' the visitor replied.

"'How big is your ocean?'

"'It's gigantic.'

"'You mean about a quarter of the size of my well here?'

"'Bigger.'

"'Bigger? You mean half as big?'

"'No, even bigger.'

"'Is it . . . as big as this well?'

"'There's no comparison.'

"'That's impossible! I've got to see this for myself.'

"The two of them set off together. When the frog from the well saw the ocean, it was such a shock that his head exploded into a million pieces."

When Pooh finished the story, he sat silently for a while, allowing me to reflect on it. Finally he said, "You see, Kat, this story is what your journey has been about. The frog from the well could not relate to something so far beyond his own experience—that is why his head exploded. Just like the frog, you had to break the bonds of your ordinary mind and become the frog who lives in the huge ocean of Buddha mind."

I was overcome. I wanted to tell Pooh what I was feeling, but I had difficulty finding the right words. Finally I said simply, "Thank you, Poohbear, for bringing me to the ocean." I stood up and went over to the couch, where I gathered him up and hugged him so tightly he squirmed to make me loosen my grasp.

"I hope you do not hug your human teachers this tightly, Kat. You could break a rib," he said. "Now if you are quite finished, I would like to go back to what you said before the story." I put him down and joined him on the couch. After he shook his fur back into place, he continued.

"You said you could not believe how much things have changed. So tell me, Kat, what exactly has changed?"

And his question became the answer. The veil between ordinary mind and Buddha mind lifted, and I saw clearly what had changed.

"*Nothing* has changed, Pooh," I replied. "Mom is still dying. Dad is still the same person he's always been. Michael and I are still struggling financially. I'm still dealing with mood swings and hot flashes. I'm not doing the work I used to love. I don't have the energy level I used to have. No *thing* has changed."

"So?"

"What has changed is that my head exploded into pieces," I said laughing, as I recalled my earlier meditation on the sofa before our conversation began. I laughed so hard that tears ran down my face. Catzenbear came running in to see what he was missing, and I grabbed him and held him as tightly as I'd held Pooh, still laughing at the thought of my head exploding like Humpty Dumpty when he fell off the wall. Unlike Humpty, however, I was coming back together again just fine, and without the help of all the king's horses and all the king's men—and without much help from Catzenbear, whose squirming was even more pronounced now, making me quickly put him down on the couch next to Poohbear.

Pooh was unmoved by my display, taking it, as usual, in his stride. I regained some composure and said, "Pooh, I'm so glad we're all going to the mountains for a week. It will be a good time for me to reflect on everything that has happened this year."

"I look forward to it, Kat. I always like seeing new places, and you are right, this will be an excellent time for you to reflect on what I have taught you."

I smiled as I got up to get dressed. *Yes indeed, nothing has changed.*

Early the next morning Michael and I packed the car, and the four of us left for the mountains. It was a long drive, and we didn't get to our rented cabin until late afternoon. We were pleased to find it was clean, roomy, and nicely furnished, with a bedroom that was actually a sleeping loft. The loft was reached by climbing a steep, narrow staircase, and the platform for the loft was supported by beams running all the way across the ceiling of the living room and kitchen. Pooh and Catz bounded up the staircase and quickly settled down on the bed to rest from the long drive. Michael and I busied ourselves with unpacking and making dinner, and after a leisurely meal, we stepped out to take a walk down the path to the river.

As I followed Michael single file on the narrow path, I became caught up in the sound of the water coursing down the middle of the river, making whitecaps as it rushed and roared over large, slippery boulders. Closer to me, the water became a babbling brook as it flowed slowly over smaller, moss-covered rocks and the piles of twigs caught between them. The sound of the soft breeze rustling through the pines captured my attention as it gently caressed my cheek.

When we got to Michael's fishing spot, I sat on the rocks and watched large fish feed on insects in the eddies, while Michael inspected the hatch of the insects to determine what type of flies he would tie that night. My vision shifted to the pines, oaks, and sycamores surrounding us with so many shades and hues of green, from the tops of the trees down to their reflection in the glassy, still areas of the water. I was very happy to be here—this place made all my senses come alive.

I picked up a handful of the rich, fertile dirt and sniffed its raw, earthy smell of leaves, grass, and moss. I was so looking forward to a longer walk the next day to further explore this glorious place.

Back at the cabin, we turned in early. It always amazed me how dark the night was when we got out of Los Angeles and into the mountains. Fortunately, someone had been considerate enough to leave a flashlight; otherwise, navigating the staircase to the sleeping loft would have been difficult, since all the light switches were downstairs.

The flashlight came in handy when, in the middle of the night, we were awakened by a loud crashing sound. Shining the light into the pitch blackness, we checked around the cabin from our perch in the loft. Seeing nothing amiss, we assumed the sound was caused by an animal outside and snuggled back down to sleep.

The next morning, Michael took off at first light to go fly-fishing. When I woke up, Pooh was still on the bed. I told him about my experience at the river and said I was going to take a nice long walk to deepen my experience with nature. He smiled and went back to sleep.

I dismissed his rather knowing attitude and went to the

bathroom to get ready for my walk. There I found Catzenbear curled up in the sink. He would often do this at home, so I thought nothing of it and just moved my little kitten onto the top of the vanity while I brushed my teeth. Then I let the water run so he could get a drink, and as soon as I turned the water off, he got back in the sink and went to sleep.

Before long, I was walking along the path beside the river. I was enjoying the fresh air, the smell of the pines, the rustling sound of the river, and the stillness of being in the country—a contrast to the constant traffic sounds of downtown Los Angeles. I hadn't realized how much I needed to be peacefully immersed in nature.

I'd been walking for about half an hour when I encountered a big batch of no-see-ums. They were everywhere, and I'd forgotten to put on insect repellant. After a few minutes of getting dive-bombed by these annoying insects, I decided to turn back, but when I started back, the no-see-ums stayed with me. I walked faster and faster, but I couldn't escape them.

Pretty soon I was running and waving my arms and hands to brush the bugs away from my ears and eyes. The whining sound was nonstop, and I was reminded of a video I'd seen of the Alaskan caribou, driven mad by mosquitoes and racing across the tundra to the ocean to escape them. I pictured what I must look like, some sort of wild-eyed Monty Python character, crashing down the path, waving my hands around madly.

I ran the whole way back and didn't escape my tormentors until I got inside the cabin. What had taken me a half-hour to walk took ten minutes to run. I was sweating and bent over, panting for breath. Pooh was downstairs on the couch and looked at me with amusement.

"I see your experience with nature was not quite what you expected," he said.

Ignoring his remark, I headed to the bathroom for a shower. I could swear I heard him chuckling as I left the room. Catzenbear was still in the sink, which seemed a little odd. At home his habit was to stay there briefly and then be out and about.

I felt much better after I got cleaned up. I sat down with Pooh and laughed about how my expectations for my walk turned out like a lot of my meditation sittings—only on the walk, my body was racing instead of my mind. I told Pooh there were many times in my sittings I would have preferred running and waving my hands in the air to staying put on my cushion.

"Speaking of running around, what's going on with Catzenbear, Pooh? Why is he staying in the sink and not up and about exploring and playing?"

"Oh, he had a bad experience last night, so he may stay in the sink for a while."

"What do you mean? … Oh no, was that the crashing sound we heard last night? Did he fall?"

"Indeed. He has not quite learned his lesson about walking in high places and on narrow beams. He took a tumble, but fortunately landed on the couch."

"Oh, poor little thing. I'd better go see how he's doing."

I went to the bathroom, picked Catzenbear up out of the sink, and held him close, stroking his head and assuring him he was not in any danger. I decided to take him to the living room, to see if perhaps he would be less afraid if I held him close and carried him into the bigger room. But his body tensed as we walked into the room, and he looked up at the ceiling rafter as though a scary monster was sitting on it. I set him down on the couch, whereupon he immediately jumped off and slunk back to the bathroom.

"I guess you're right, Pooh. He needs more time to recover.

I'm surprised Catzenbear didn't learn his lesson after his fall from the roof garden."

"You must remember Catzenbear is still a kitten, and although he possesses Buddha nature, he has not yet blossomed into the discernment Buddha mind brings. Catzenbear will slowly put the pieces together and learn to be more circumspect in life, just as you have learned from your own falls and follies, Kat."

I acknowledged Pooh's assessment with a smile, and he continued.

"Taking the time to reflect, as we talked about doing while we are here, is of the utmost importance. As I have said many times, reflecting on one's experiences, both in meditation and in life, is what brings wisdom and judgment."

Pooh tilted his head toward the bathroom. "Catzenbear used neither wisdom nor judgment, nor did he take time to reflect before he fell again. There are many times Catzenbear provides such examples and contributes greatly to my ability as a teacher." Pooh stretched to his full length as if he were looking for a positive memory, and then said, "Ah yes, remember how Catzenbear concentrates and becomes so absorbed as he watches the water swirling down the bathtub drain?"

"Sure. I use that visual of him to stay focused when I find myself falling asleep as I go into deeper states of meditation." Then, thinking of my kitten's fall from the rafter, I couldn't resist the pun. "So is that why Catzenbear is hiding out in the bathroom sink? He's reflecting on his 'heightened' experience?"

Pooh grinned. "That was clever, Kat. I enjoy your humor most when it is not leveled at me. You are absolutely correct—this is exactly what Catzenbear is doing in the sink. He is reflecting on what he did to create such a frightful experience and is building up his courage to go back out into the big bad world. I think he is unlikely to have to do it a third time before he learns. Do you agree?"

"I certainly hope so," I said, as an astonishing feeling of joy washed over me. It was wonderful to share a joke and be acknowledged as an equal by my teacher. I closed my eyes for a moment just to honor the immense feeling of gratitude I was experiencing.

When I opened my eyes, Poohbear was on his way to the kitchen, and I realized that since I'd started out for my walk so early, we hadn't yet had breakfast. I followed him and put the kettle on for tea, then fixed some cereal for me and a bowl of cat food for him, and one for Catz, which I took to the bathroom and placed next to the sink.

After we finished eating, I washed the dishes and went upstairs to the sleeping loft to get my journal. I looked at the rafters as I climbed back down, astonished once again at Catzenbear's decision to walk on the four-inch-wide beams last night.

Pooh was back on the couch, and I sat down beside him. "I thought this might be a good time for me to reflect on what I've learned from our journey over the past year."

"By all means, Kat. I am very pleased to see that you understand how important this is." Pooh smiled approvingly.

"Thank you. I've given this some thought and narrowed it down to what I feel are the most important lessons," I began. "As a result of developing tolerance for the strong feelings that come up in my meditations, I've been able to examine more closely the stories behind them. Now I can see how I create my world by holding on to those stories and my beliefs about them. Also, I'm more open to my experiences in meditation, and I am actually curious about what is at the source of those experiences."

Pooh nodded, "Indeed, curiosity is of utmost importance

in a meditation practice, followed closely by courage and commitment to stay the course."

I laughed. "Now you sound like the corporate trainer I used to be, Pooh, creating a list of words beginning with the same letter so it's easier to remember them. Okay. Curiosity, courage, commitment: the three Cs. Got it."

"Good," Pooh replied. "Go on."

"I know you're going to like this one," I grinned. "I need to let go of expectations—not only about how my sittings should go but also about how something as simple as a walk in the woods should go."

Pooh laughed. "Well Kat, you only said you were going to deepen your experience with nature, you did not say how. On a more serious note, I have observed your progress in this area. You are much better about letting your sittings unfold. It has been some time since you complained about things not going the way you wanted them to."

"Now that you say it, Pooh, I realize just how much I really have changed. When I think back, it seems like all I ever did was complain about how my practice was going. I don't do that much anymore."

I paused and closed my eyes for a moment to think. "I want to say something about feeling joy, but I'm not sure how to express it. I'm feeling joyful much of the time now, and I think the reason is I've learned that what is happening in my life is not the determining factor for whether I can feel joy. It isn't what is happening outside, it is what is happening inside that counts. How I view life, things, people—all of it—that's what makes the difference between joy or sorrow." I was feeling excited to share these thoughts, having them come alive as I spoke. "I don't have to do anything or achieve anything to feel joyful. The more I let go, the more I can naturally just *be*. Our little slogan, 'If you cannot be, you cannot do' is a great reminder for me when I get caught up in my busy-ness."

"Excellent, Kat. I very much like that little saying myself. 'Be not Do,' or 'Being *is* Doing.' This could go on and on," he said, smiling. "Is there anything else?"

I got up to get a glass of water and pace for a moment. "There is one area that is still a big challenge for me, Pooh. Now that I am back at work, I find it difficult to stay in my Buddha mind for the whole day. It is too easy to slip back to ordinary-mind thinking. Here is an example of what I mean. I was really busy one day, working at warp speed, when an Avon executive walked by my desk. I said hello and she completely ignored me, which sent me into a tailspin of stories about who I used to be: *How dare she treat me like that! Doesn't she know who I am?* This one little incident affected me for hours. Any suggestions about how I can stay more mindful during the workday?"

"It is very difficult to remain mindful when you are interacting with many people in a fast-paced environment, Kat. You are wise to ask for help with this. Are there any opportunities for you to go and meditate for a few minutes during the day?"

"Not in my present situation. Back in the days when I had my own office, that wouldn't have been a problem, but there is no place I can go to be alone during the day at Avon or at the agency office."

Poohbear sat up straighter and asked again, "Are you sure there is no place you can go to be alone? Do you drive to work?"

I looked at him in astonishment. "I can't believe I didn't think of that. Of course, I could sit in my car and meditate for a little while during lunch."

Pooh grinned. "Glad to be of assistance, Kat. One other idea. No matter how busy you are, you can occasionally take a minute for a couple of deep breaths and observe what your mind is doing."

Now I grinned. "You got me, Pooh. I do know how to do this. I'm just not confident I can remember to do it when I'm interacting with people all day. I know what I'll do. I'll set the silent alarm on my watch to buzz every hour and remind me to stop and do my quick, deep-breathing meditation to find out where my mind is."

"Excellent, Kat. The idea of an hourly reminder is a good idea. I am quite pleased with your progress. Your reflections about what you have learned show that you have reached a level of wisdom and understanding about your practice."

Pooh got up and shook himself all over. He narrowed his glance and asked with a note of finality, "Kat, why do you think reaching this new level in your practice is so important?"

I sat back down on the couch and thought about this for a moment. "Well, Pooh, it seems to me I am now at a point where I can trust my own inner wisdom instead of relying so much on my teachers." I felt a bit self-conscious having said this, knowing how Pooh felt about me striking out on my own too quickly. "This is not to say I still don't have much to learn. But now, when I take time to reflect on my experiences, both in meditation and in my life, I can access a level of wisdom and understanding that allows me to make adjustments on my own."

Pooh nodded encouragingly at what I had said. "Yes Kat, this is exactly what I have been trying to teach you—wisdom and understanding are the antidotes to delusion and ignorance. When you develop this level of understanding, you are able to tolerate, analyze, and adjust the views that inform your behavior."

"I am beginning to realize that I am no longer a slave to my ordinary mind." I became a little teary-eyed as I went on. "I don't mean to get sappy with you, Pooh, but I could never have made this journey without your teaching and support."

"I know, Kat. We were destined to take this journey together. That is why I am here, and why Catzenbear is here. But this is only the beginning. Our journey is far from over. We will have many more adventures together."

He got up and walked to the corner of the couch, where he curled up, wrapping his big plume of a tail around him. He looked up at me and said, "We have been at this for some time, and I am quite tired. It is time for a nap." With that he settled down, put a paw over his eyes to block the light, and quickly fell asleep.

I sat reflecting on our discussion. I had indeed been gaining wisdom and understanding. I knew this was true, and yet I felt a little disappointed, as though somehow this special moment of acknowledgment should have been bigger, more ceremonious.

I decided to meditate for a while. Wrapping my shawl around me, I closed my eyes and allowed my thoughts and feelings to pass by like lazy clouds moving through a clear blue sky. As thoughts dropped away, I sat for some time in a state of total equanimity. I was conscious and alert, and yet I was not thinking. I'd read that such a state of being was possible, and here it was. I let it flow through me, around me. *So this is my ceremony, my celebration—the experience of no thoughts for a brief period of time.* And somehow, it was enough.

As I returned to a more conscious state, I sat for a while simply feeling my breath going in and out before I opened my eyes. I looked over at Poohbear sleeping peacefully. Pleasantly tired myself, I stretched out and put my head on the cushion next to him. Then I drifted off into a deep and dreamless sleep, lying there next to a Buddha Master cat on a sofa in a small cabin in the woods, with Michael outside fishing and a Buddha nature kitten in the bathroom sink—*all as it should be.*

And my journey had only just begun.

THE FOUR NOBLE TRUTHS IN A NUTSHELL

The Buddha was an optimist.
Okay, so he did say life was filled with suffering.
But notice he didn't say you personally have to suffer.
He only said life was filled with suffering.

Look around you.
Do you not see suffering?

The Buddha also said we can know the cause of suffering.
And fortunately, the cause is close at hand.

This is excellent news.
Because the Buddha said there is a way out.
And he provided a pretty cool path.

But first, the cause.
How can we know it?

The Buddha gave us a map.
It's called meditation.

Kat Tansey
2007

ACKNOWLEDGMENTS

I AM fortunate to have an author, editor, and sister wrapped into one person. Revising a manuscript can be an arduous process, but working with my sister, Patricia Heller, made it a remarkable experience. Patricia would ever so gently point out when I'd dropped into ordinary mind writing and nudge me back into Buddha mind prose.

My meditation teacher, Jason Siff, opened up the world of Buddhist meditation for me. I could not have found a better guide to help me learn how to access what I refer to as my Buddha mind.

Always a loving presence who embodies what I call Buddha nature, Jacquelin Siff welcomed me to Buddhist meditation with compassion and friendship and was a constant source of encouragement for me during my first few years of practice

Love for the dharma (teachings of the Buddha) and generosity of spirit were embodied by Gordon Smith. I was very fortunate to be part of the sangha (meditation group) made possible by Gordon, and though he is no longer part of this physical world, he will always be in my heart.

My brother Jack Kimbell has always been appreciative of my writing. His continued encouragement over the years has meant a lot to me, and I value our relationship more than mere words can express.

My former husband, Michael Tansey, supported me in many ways during my struggle with chronic fatigue syndrome and depression. His allergies to ordinary cats led us to discover our allergy-free Maine Coon cats, Buddha Master Pooh, and the embodiment of Buddha nature, Catzenbear.

My therapist, Dr. Leanne Watt, at a time when most psychologists were not knowledgeable about the value of Buddhist meditation, encouraged my meditation practice as part of our therapeutic work, and our work together was much the richer for it.

My friend Cathy Palochko read an early version and then formatted the first three chapters into a design that looked like a real book. This visual symbol kept me going through the many months of writing and rewriting.

I was delighted when Findhorn Press decided to publish this new edition of *Choosing to Be*. It has been my dream to reach a global audience with this book, and becoming part of the Findhorn group of authors has helped me fulfill that dream.

My heartfelt thanks go to Thierry Bogliolo at Findhorn Press for sharing my vision and bringing my book on board, and to Damian Keenan for our beautiful bright new cover that will be sure to catch the reader's eye in the bookstores!

None of this would have been possible were it not for my partner, Greg Narog. I am fortunate to have finally found my true companion. As our journey continues to unfold, I am increasingly grateful for his extraordinary wisdom, integrity, compassion, and love.

I deeply appreciate all the authors, practitioners, and meditation teachers who have shared their wisdom with me. I have benefited greatly from their writings and have taken their teachings to heart. *Choosing to Be* is my interpretation of what I have learned from them and from my own practice, made into a

Acknowledgments

story, and is not intended to represent with authority the views of my teachers and the authors I have referenced.

And finally, to the magic of Gridley Road in Ojai, California, where I walked day after day and spoke the early drafts of this book into my handheld tape recorder. Just walking on Gridley Road is a meditation.

FURTHER READING

Overview of Buddhism

For those readers who are new to Buddhist teachings, there are many books that provide an overview of the history and the various forms of Buddha dharma (the teachings). The one below is quite accessible for newcomers.

Samuel Bercholz and Sherab Chodzin Kohn,
Entering the Stream:
An Introduction to the Buddha and His Teachings.

Meditation Instruction

The form of meditation I practice has evolved from my early years of study with Jason Siff and my own readings on Vipassana Meditation, which is part of the Theravada tradition, based on the Buddha's teachings in India some 2600 years ago.

To learn more about his teaching, read articles, and find out about his retreats, visit the Skillful Meditation Project website at www.SkillfulMeditation.org.

Jason's book, *Unlearning Meditation*, which is published by Shambhala Publications, has received endorsements from well-known authors and meditation teachers Jack Kornfield, Joseph Goldstein, Joan Halifax, and Stephen Batchelor.

"A wise, practical, and radical book that sheds new and wondrous light on dharma in the West."
—Joan Halifax, author of *Being with Dying*

"Jason Siff is one of the most distinctive and engaging voices of the emerging Buddhist culture in the West."
—Stephen Batchelor, author of *Confession of a Buddhist Atheist.*

BIBLIOGRAPHY

Beck, Charlotte Joko. *Everyday Zen: Love and Work*. New York: Harper Collins, 1989.

Beck, Charlotte Joko. *Nothing Special: Living Zen*. San Francisco: Harper San Francisco, 1993.

Bercholz, Samuel and Kohn, Sherab Chodzin. *Entering the Stream: An Introduction to the Buddha and His Teachings*. Boston: Shambala, 1993.

Bodhi, Bhikku and Nanamoli, Bhikkhu. *The Middle Length Discourse of the Buddha: Translation of the Majjhima Nikaya*. Boston: Wisdom Publications, 1995.

Boorstein, Sylvia. *It's Easier Than You Think: The Buddhist Way to Happiness*. San Francisco: Harper San Francisco, 1995.

Buddhist Publication Society. "Taming the Mind: Discourses of the Buddha." The Wheel No. 51. Kandy, Sri Lanka, BPS Online Edition, 2006.

Epstein, Mark, *Thoughts Without A Thinker*. New York: Basic Books, 1995.

Gethers, Peter. *The Cat Who'll Live Forever: The Final Adventures of Norton, the Perfect Cat, and His Imperfect Human*. New York: Broadway, 2001.

Chodron, Pema. *The Wisdom of No Escape*. Boston: Shambhala Publications, 1991.

Goddard, Dwight. *A Buddhist Bible*. Boston: Beacon Press, 1970.

Goldstein, Joseph. *Insight Meditation: The Practice of Freedom*. Boston: Shambhala Publications, 1993.

Gunaratana, Mahathera Henepola. *The Jhanas In Theravada Buddhist Meditation*. Kandy: Buddhist Publication Society, 1988.

Hanh, Thich Nhat. *Peace Is Every Step: The Path of Mindfulness in Everyday Life*. New York: Bantam Books, 1991.

Hanh, Thich Nhat. *The Miracle of Mindfulness: A Manual on Meditation*. Boston: Beacon Press, 1975.

Hart, William. *Vipassana Meditation as Taught by S.N. Goenka*. San Francisco: Harper San Francisco, 1987.

Heller, Patricia. *If You Hear the Message Three Times, Listen*. Charlottesville, VA: Hampton Roads Publishing, 2004.

Hornidge, Marilis. *That Yankee Cat: The Maine Coon*. Gardiner, Maine: Tilbury House, 1981.

Kabat-Zinn, Jon. *Wherever You Go, There You Are: Mindfulness Meditation in Everyday Life*. New York: Hyperion, 1994.

Kaviratna, Harischandra, Trans. *Dhammapada: Wisdom of the Buddha*. Pasadena, CA: Theosophical University Press, 1980.

Khema, Ayya. *Being Nobody, Going Nowhere: Meditations on the Buddhist Path*. Boston: Wisdom Publications, 1987.

Kornfield, Jack. *A Path with Heart: A Guide Through the Perils and Promises of Spiritual Life*. New York: Bantam Books, 1993.

Lama Surya Das. *Letting Go of the Person You Used to Be: Lessons on Change, Loss, and Spiritual Transformation*. New York: Broadway Books, 2003.

Levine, Stephen. *A Gradual Awakening*. New York: Anchor Books, 1979.

Masson, Jeffrey Moussaieff. *The Nine Emotional Lives of Cats: A Journey into the Feline Heart*. New York: Ballantine Books, 2002.

Nyanatiloka. *The Word of the Buddha: An Outline of the Teaching of The Buddha*. Kandy, Sri Lanka: Buddhist Publication Society, 1967.

Page, Tony, ed. and Yamamoto, Kosho, trans. *The Mahaparinirvana Sutra in Twelve Volumes*, Vol.3, pg.1. Nirvana Publications, London, 2000.

Rinpoche, Sogyal. *The Tibetan Book of Living and Dying*. San Francisco: Harper San Francisco, 1992.

Salzberg, Sharon. *Lovingkindness: The Revolutionary Art of Happiness*. Boston: Shambhala Publications, 2002.

Siff, Jason. *Unlearning Meditation*, Boston: Shambhala Publications, 2010.

Suzuki, Shunryu. *Zen Mind, Beginner's Mind: Informal Talks on Zen Meditation and Practice*. New York: Weatherhill, 1970.

Thera, Nyanaponika, trans. "The Five Mental Hindrances and Their Conquest." The Wheel No. 26. Kandy, Sri Lanka: British Publication Society, 1993.

Thera, Nyanaponika. *The Heart of Buddhist Meditation*. New York: Samuel Weiser, 1965.

Thera, Nyanaponika. *The Vision of Dhamma*. UK: Century Hutchinson Publishing, 1986.

Tolle, Eckhart. *The Power of Now: A Guide to Spiritual Enlightenment*. Novato, CA: New World Library, 1999.

Universal Buddhist Cultural Service. *The Story of the Buddha*. Rosemead, California, 2000.

Yazinuma, Yoshiyuki. *Zen Cats*. New York: Abbeville Press, 2001.

SOURCES FOR QUOTATIONS

Front Cover:

From the book *The Power of Now,* © 1999 by Eckhart Tolle, p.109. Reprinted with permission of New World Library, Novato, CA, www.newworldlibrary.com.

Chapter One: Deciding to Stay

From *The Tibetan Book of Living and Dying* by Soygal Rinpoche, © 1993 by Rigpa Fellowship, p.49. Reprinted by permission from Harper Collins Publishers.

Wordsworth, William, "Ode: Intimations of Immortality from Recollections of Early Childhood," Stanza V. From *English Romantic Poets*, © 1961 by James Stephens, Edwin Beck, Royall Snow, p. 64.

Chapter Two: Building the Team

From *The Mahaparinirvana Sutra in Twelve Volumes,* edited by Dr. Tony Page, Vol.3, pg.1. Used with permission of Dr. Tony Page.

Chapter Three: Just Sitting

From *Zen Mind, Beginner's Mind*, by Shunryu Suzuki, 1993, p.49. Protected under terms of the International Copyright Union. Reprinted by arrangement with Shambhala Publications, Inc, www.Shambhala.com.

Chapter Four: Finding Joy

From *Nothing Special: Living Zen*, © 1993 by Charlotte Joko Beck, p.232. Reprinted by permission from Harper Collins Publishers.

From *Everyday Zen: Love and Work*, © 1989 by Charlotte Joko Beck, p.1. Reprinted by permission from Harper Collins Publishers.

Chapter Five: Walking on Our Toes

From *Peace is Every Step,* © 1991 by Thich Nhat Hanh, p.28. Used by permission of Bantam Books, a division of Random House, Inc.

Chapter Six: Dealing with Dogs

From *Insight Meditation*, © 1993 by Joseph Goldstein, p.57. Reprinted with arrangement with Shambhala Publications Inc., www.Shambhala.com.

Chapter Seven: Letting Go of Tuna

From *A Path with Heart*, © 1993 by Jack Kornfield, p.86. Used by permission of Bantam Books, a division of Random House, Inc.

Chapter Eight: Lovingkindness

From *Being Nobody, Going Nowhere*, © 1987 by Ayya Khema, p.41. Used with permission from Wisdom Publications, www.wisdompublications.org.

From *Lovingkindness* by Sharon Salzberg, p.23, © by Sharon Salzberg. Reprinted by arrangement with Shambhala Publications, Inc., www.Shambhala.com.

Chapter Nine: Watching the Water

From *A Path with Heart*, © 1993 by Jack Kornfield, p. 95. Used by permission of Bantam Books, a division of Random House, Inc.

Chapter Ten: Catzenbear's Tranquility

From *The Five Mental Hindrances and Their Conquest: Sumyutta Nikaya 46:53*. Translation by Thera Nyanaponika, 1993. Reprinted with permission from The Buddhist Publication Society.

Chapter Eleven: Poohbear's Rapture

From *The Five Mental Hindrances and Their Conquest: Samannaphala Sutta, Digha Nikaya No. 2*. Translation by Thera Nyanaponika, 1993. Reprinted with permission from The Buddhist Publication Society.

Chapter Twelve: Gaining Wisdom

From *The Wisdom of No Escape* by Pema Chodron, © 1991 by Pema Chodron, p.42. Reprinted by arrangement with Shambhala Publications, Inc., www.Shambhala.com.

From *The Tibetan Book of Living and Dying* by Sogyal Rinpoche, © 1993 by Rigpa Fellowship, p.41. Reprinted by permission from Harper Collins Publishers.

ABOUT THE AUTHOR

Kat Tansey is a magical storyteller who shares her soul, expands our minds, and reveals to us our inner wisdom. She has been a meditation practitioner for twenty years and has enjoyed a unique relationship with cats since she was a little girl.

After twenty years in the high-pressure worlds of corporate consulting, Kat was struck down by chronic fatigue syndrome as she began her book tour for *Winning the Change Game*, a book about implementing organizational change. She spent years recovering and getting back into life, and her journey to regain her physical, emotional, and spiritual health was the genesis for *Choosing to Be*.

Kat and her partner Greg Narog live in Ojai, California.

Poohbear became part of Kat's life at Christmas of 1989, and Catzenbear joined them in the spring of 1993. The picture of three of them above was Kat's first Ojai Christmas card in 1995. It was cut and pasted together because when the photographer came to take the Christmas pictures no one would cooperate.

INNER TRANQUILITY
A Guide to Seated Meditation

by Darren Main

This down-to-earth primer on meditation is a newly revised and expanded version of *The Findhorn Book of Meditation*, written by popular San Francisco yoga and meditation teacher Darren Main, author of *Yoga and the Path of an Urban Mystic*. Eschewing religious jargon, it is the perfect beginner's guide for western yogis interested in a practical and pan-spiritual approach to working with the mind for optimum health. Drawing on the mystic heart of all spiritual traditions and modern 12-step recovery programs advocating personal responsibility and group support, this small book has a big message: personal commitment to daily practice brings results. Split into two parts—Learning How to Meditate and How Meditation Works—with a large appendix detailing Frequently Asked Questions, Styles of Meditation, and Props and Supplies, *Inner Tranquility* covers the bases, from practicalities of when, where, and how to the latest neuroscientific information about why meditation works. Its refreshingly modern take on an ancient healing tradition and accessible language is sure to attract many new practitioners.

ISBN 978-1-84409-503-2

FINDHORN PRESS

Life Changing Books

For a complete catalogue, please contact:

Findhorn Press
117-121 High Street
Forres IV36 1AB
Scotland, UK
t +44(0)1309 690582
f +44(0)131 777 2711
e info@findhornpress.com

or consult our catalogue online (with secure order facility):
www.findhornpress.com

For information on the Findhorn Foundation:
www.findhorn.org